NEW POETRY
IN HINDI

D1563357

Anthem South Asian Studies

Series editor: Crispin Bates

NEW POETRY IN HINDI

Nayi Kavita

An Anthology

edited, translated and introduced by
Lucy Rosenstein

Anthem Press
London

This edition first published by Anthem Press 2004

Anthem Press is an imprint of
Wimbledon Publishing Company
75-76 Blackfriars Road
London SE1 8HA
or
PO Box 9779, London SW19 7QA

This edition first published in 2002 by
Permanent Black, Delhi, India.

British Library Cataloguing in Publication Data
Data available

Library of Congress in Publication Data
A catalogue record has been applied for

1 3 5 7 9 10 8 6 4 2

ISBN 1 84331 124 0 (Hbk)
ISBN 1 84331 125 9 (Pbk)

Typeset by Pentagon Graphics Pvt. Ltd, India
Printed in India

CONTENTS

To my Grandfather who taught me the power of the Word
To my Mother and my Brother who introduced me to poetry
To Kolyo who left his poems behind

ACKNOWLEDGEMENTS

It has taken me five years to cover the distance from my first rather vague vision of a book on Hindi incarnation of 'New Poetry' to this anthology. This journey has been at times enjoyable, at times exasperating. On the way I met many co-travellers who helped me to reach my destination: some supplied me with provisions, some showed me the way, some kept me company. I am indebted to all of them, not only for taking me to my goal, but also for making the journey itself memorable and meaningful.

I am grateful to the School of Oriental and African Studies and to the British Academy for giving me research grants which made my fieldwork trips to India possible. A grant from the SOAS Publications Committee contributed towards the production costs. SOAS also granted me two terms of research leave which gave me precious time to read, think and write.

My deepest gratitude goes to Rupert Snell and Richard Gombrich for their unfailing support, their perceptive criticism and editorial help. Rupert Snell not only painstakingly commented on my writing, but also spent endless hours helping me to format the book. I would like to thank Natasha Ahmad for all the time and effort she put into the compilation of the first draft of the glossary. Rachel Harrison was always there to answer my questions on English idiom.

I was fortunate to meet half of the poets included in this anthology and to work closely with some of them. Kunwar Narain participated in the translation of his poetry to such an extent that, if I were not concerned about burdening him with the responsibility for my mistakes, I would call him a cotranslator. Moreover, he and Bharati–ji made me feel at home in Delhi. Jyotsna Milan provided me with her collections of poems and spent many hours talking to me and commenting on my translations. She, Ramesh Chandra Shah, Shampa and Rajula gave me a warm welcome in Bhopal. Amitra Bharati offered me both her hospitality in Lucknow, and a friendship I treasure enormously. Pawan Mathur provided me with his mother's collections and facilitated my contact with her since she was too unwell to meet me personally. Prabha and Badrivishal Pitti generously sent me the material related to Kanta and commented on my translations of her poetry. Kedarnath Singh made the time to meet me and look at my translations of his verses.

There are many more friends and acquaintances in India to whom I would like to give my warmest thanks. My Allahabad guru-ji, Ram Swarup Chaturvedi, met me every day for weeks on end to discuss my draft translations, refusing to accept payment for his time and effort. Mohan Avasthi, Shri Prakash Shukla, Nilabh and Satya Prakash Mishra also spent many monsoon mornings discussing Hindi poetry with me. Ranjana Kakkar welcomed me in her home in Allahabad and looked after me, with Raju's help, like an older sister. Vandana and Arvind Mehrotra extended their kindness, warmth and friendship to me. The staff at the Sahitya Sammelan library allowed me access to all the material I needed and photocopied countless pages at my request. Pankaj Mishra gave me shelter in Delhi every time I needed one. Gagan Gill supported me as a friend in moments of despair, presented me with all Amrita Bharati's books, and organised my meeting with her. Ashok Vajpeyi gave me a chance to discuss my views on modernity in Hindi poerty with a Delhi audience. Rustam Singh and Rajkamal Prakashan helped me find the addresses of copyrightholders. Rukun Advani painstakingly edited my manuscript. Somadeva Vasudeva selflessly agreed to help me with the formatting of the book and transformed my amateurish attempts at typesetting into an elegant, professional CRC.

Last but not least, Peter accompanied me for most of this journey, even when it lay through thorny thickets and up steep hills. To all these people I offer my heartfelt gratitude.

Lucy Rosenstein

NOTE ON TRANSLITERATION
AND ABBREVIATIONS

The standard method for transliterating *Devanāgarī* has been adopted for all Hindi terms and titles of works. The transliteration font used is Normyn. Inherent *-a* has been written when following a conjunct. Vowel nasalisation is indicated with a tilde above the vowel, consonant nasalisation with the relevant nasal. The font used for the Hindi poems is Jaisalmer. Names of writers, places and publishers have been anglicized; preference has been given to spellings already in use.

The following abbreviations and signs have been used in the *Glossary*:

adj.	adjective
adj. (f.)	adjective with a feminine ending
conj.	conjunct
encl.	enclitic
f.	feminine
f./m.	used for words with double gender
interj.	interjection
m.	masculine
ppn.	postposition
pron.	pronoun
vi.	intransitive verb
vt.	transitive verb
:	divides a literal meaning from the meaning in the context
→	therefore
?	headword not found in any dictionary. Meaning conjectured.

COPYRIGHT STATEMENT

I would like to thank the following for permission to reprint material which they published originally, or for which they hold copyright.

- Mrs Ila Dalmia for the following (extracts) of poems by Agyeya: 'Dūrvācal', 'Usā-darśan', 'Rāt mẽ gā̃v, 'Cup-cāp' Śiśir kā bhor', 'Nanda devī 14', 'Asādhya vīnā, 'Kālemegdān' 'Jo pul banāyẽ ge' and 'Narak kī samasyā';

- Mrs Shanta Muktibodh for the following (extracts of) poems by Muktibodh: 'Āhere mẽ', 'Cā̃d kā muh terhā hai' and 'Becain cīl';

- Dr Ranjana Argade for the following poems by Shamsher Bahadur Singh: 'Ek pīlī śām', 'Usā' 'Pūrnimā kā cā̃d,' 'Subah', 'Dhūp kothrī ke āine mẽ kharī', 'Preyasī', 'Tumne mujhe' and 'Kavi ghāghol detā hai';

- Mrs Vimaleshwari Sahay for the following poems by Raghuvir Sahay: 'Āj phir se śurū huā', 'Pānī ke samsmaran', 'Maidān mẽ', 'Seb becnā', Akelī aurat', 'Manusya-machlī yuddha', 'Vyāvahārik log' and 'Phūt';

- Kunwar Narain for 'Kamre mẽ dhūp', 'Antim ũ caī', 'Bāqī kavitā', 'Dūr tak', 'Ek saṅksipta kālkhanda mẽ', 'Badalte postar', 'Kabūtar aur billī' and 'Prem kā rog';

- Kedarnath Singh for 'Bāzār', Akāl mẽ sāras', 'Ānā', 'Kuch aur tukre', 'Sukhī ādmī', 'Bāgh 6' and 'Maīne Gaṅgā ko dekhā';

- Shakunt Mathur for 'Nigāhõ ne kahā', 'Tum sundar ho, ghar sundar ho', Kāfī Hāūs', Kā̃c', 'Cunautī', 'Sahnā', 'Chotī chotī bātẽ' and Cilkā jhīl';

- Prabha for the following poems by Kanta: 'Dhuā̃', 'Sukh', 'Dūb gaye haī saṅket', 'Dīvārõ par dīvārẽ', 'Rod-laimp kā mandā mandā ālok', 'Dhūp camak rahī thī', 'Halkī-halkī lālimā, 'Ākāś, aur ākāś ke bīc', 'Ādhere-sī chā gayī hũ', 'Prthvī ko pairõ tale raũdtā', 'Bacce kī bā̃hõ-sā maclā', 'Pratīksā', 'Go, yah sac', 'Dukh to ek gandh' and 'Pahar kar lenā hai pār';

- Amrita Bharati for 'Ek cal rahī bhūmikā', Dūsrā savāl', 'Vahī ek ghatnā', 'Sannāte mẽ dūr tak', 'Man ruk gayā vahā̃', 'Lekin', and 'Śabda kī śānti mẽ';

- Jyotsna Milan for 'Is tarah hone ke bare mẽ', 'Āsmān', 'Lagātār', 'Pair', 'Pīche', 'Talāś', 'Aurat' 'Śabda', 'Artha', 'Rāt', 'Sāth-sāth āine mẽ', 'Kisī dūsrī jagah' and 'Vah'.

The author, who owns copyright on this book and takes full responsibility for all material contained within it, has made every effort to approach all copyrightholders. Perceived omissions, if reported to the author via the publisher, will be rectified in future printings.

INTRODUCTION

On the most general level this anthology is for lovers of poetry who would like to take a stroll in the landscape of Hindi verse. With the help of the English translations within it they can experience Hindi poetry even if they do not have recourse to the language of the original. The Hindi originals are included for those who know some Hindi but lack the confidence to undertake the journey into its poetry alone. The English translations and subsidiary material are provided to guide them and map their route.

When I first set off on this journey as a student of Hindi and Hindi literature, I kept getting lost. The landscape was so lush and the signposts so few and far between that I was totally disoriented. I needed a map, and since there was no study of Hindi poetry which could serve as one I set out to produce it myself.

Poetry started being written in *modern* Hindi[1] only at the beginning of the twentieth century. Before that poems were composed in different dialects of Hindi, which we sometimes label with the umbrella term Medieval Hindi.[2] They are: old Rajasthani, a language in which narrative verses and epics were written probably from the 14th century onward by the court poets of the Rajput kings to glorify their patrons; 'holy man's jargon' (*sādhukkāṛī bhāṣā*) used by popular religious poets known as *sants*, who, in the 14th–15th centuries, started singing the glory of an attributeless, formless, nameless God and denounced empty ritual and caste inequality; Maithili, a dialect of Bihar, in which the 14th-century poet Vidyapati celebrated the love between Lord Krishna and his divine consort Radha; Avadhi, from the late 14th-century onward a powerful vehicle of Sufism—the tradition of Islamic mysticism. Being the dialect of the area around Ayodhya, the supposed birth place of Lord Ram, Avadhi became also the carrier of devotion to Ram, especially in the famous 16th-century *Rāmāyana* written by Tulsidas. The last, and perhaps the most important, of the Medieval Hindi dialects was Braj Bhasha, the language spoken around Mathura, and thus the chief vehicle of devotion to Krishna, who is believed to have been born there.

As we can see, religious devotion (*bhakti*) was the focus of poetry in North India from the 14th century onwards. In the 17th century courtly love started competing for that place. *Bhakti*'s rival was *rīti*, a formalist tradition which cultivated technical virtuosity while limiting poetry's content to the world of idealised love, where the description of the beauty of the heroine from head to toe (*nakh śikh*) and classifications of different types of heroines (*nāyikā-bhed*) became popular topics. Both *bhakti* and *rīti* promoted a poetic standard according to which poets had to elaborate on a 'basic cell' or 'germ motive' (Rubin 1993, p.3) which were set for them. Their artistry was measured by their technical skill; individuality was expressed mainly by peculiarities of style. Subjectivity and originality, which are such important criteria for poetic achievement today, had little significance in a culture where poets had traditionally been regarded as seers–mediators of a higher authority rather than individual voices.

Both poetic medium and subject matter changed at the beginning of the 20th century. The shift of idiom was traumatic—the existence of highly sophisticated poetry in Braj Bhasha made its replacement with Khari Boli Hindi problematic. Being a language in its infancy, Khari Boli Hindi did not have the melodiousness, elegance of diction and prosody, and wealth of cultural associations of Braj, a language refined by several hundred years of tradition. Thus the idea of using Khari Boli for verse was anathema to poetry connoisseurs at the end of the 19th and beginning of the 20th century.

However, the onset of modernity was forcing poetry to leave behind the idealised worlds of divine lovers such as Radha and Krishna, and of courtly heroes and heroines, making it turn to the imperfect world of human concerns. For this, poetry needed a new idiom. Mahavirprasad Dwivedi, a man of modern sensibility and a champion of modern Hindi, founded the magazine *Sarasvatī* in 1900 and as its editor embarked on a 17-year crusade for the Hindi cause. He encouraged the composition of poetry in Hindi dedicated to nationalism and social reform. Dwivedi played such an important role in the establishment of modern Hindi as a literary language that this period in the development of Hindi literature (1900–18) is often called the Dwivedi *yug*, the age of Dwivedi.

Maithilisharan Gupta's *Bhārat-bhāratī*, 'The voice of India',[3] a nostalgic evocation of the past glory of India, is one of the most renowned poems of the period. A short extract gives a sufficient idea of the general tenor of this ambitious work.[4]

भारत वर्ष की श्रेष्ठता

भू-लोक गौरव, प्रकृति का पुण्य लीला स्थल कहाँ ?
फैला मनोहर गिरि हिमालय और गंगाजल जहाँ ।
सम्पूर्ण देशों से अधिक किस देश का उत्कर्ष है?
उसका कि जो ऋषिभूमि है, वह कौन ? भारतवर्ष है ॥१४ ॥
हां, वृद्ध भारतवर्ष ही संसार का सिरमौर है,
ऐसा पुरातन देश कोई विश्व में क्या और है ?
(Gupta 1920, p.4)

India's excellence

Where is earth's pride, place of Nature's sacred play?
Where the charming Himalayas and the Ganges lay.
In the whole world, which country is most excellent?
Which is it? It is India, the seer's land.
Yes, old India is the universe's crest,
Is there such an ancient country among the rest?

Similarly, another famous work of the Dwivedi *yug*, Shridhar Pathak's *Bhāratgīt*, 'Songs of India', urges:

'दुष्कृत कोई न कर तू , करते सुकृत न डर तू'
'हर कर किसी के धन को अपना भवन न भर तू'
'पर-हित के साधने में कोई न कर कसर तू' –
शुभ कर्म की तरफ़ यों सबको झुका रहा है
भारत हमारा जग को क्या क्या सिखा रहा है
(Pathak 1918, p.38)

'Do no evil deed, fear not good deed'
'Do not plunder others' wealth for your need'
'Work with dedication for others' benefit'–
This is what our India teaches mankind
How it compels one and all to be kind.

It is not difficult to see why McGregor cautiously suggests that *Bhārat-bhāratī*, which 'has perhaps little poetic quality. . . should be seen [as an example] of the use of verse for social and political discussion' (McGregor 1974, p.109), or why Poulos labels the poetry of the Dwivedi *yug* 'versified propaganda' (Schomer 1983, p.12): it is verse of public statement; its language is functional but aesthetically unappealing. Earnest, concerned with social issues and moral values, it is puritanical poetry in which aesthetic considerations are secondary. Imagination, originality, poetic sensibility and expression are wanting, the metre is restrictive, the idiom clumsy.

However, to do justice to this important period, which laid the foundations of modern Hindi poetry, one has to acknowledge that the verses written in the Dwivedi *yug* show the poets' sensitivity to the imperatives of the time. The preference for didacticism in their verses reflects the culture of its audience—the Hindu middle class—marked by the puritanism of both the Arya Samaj[5] and the British Victorianism. Moreover the lack of sophistication and the inelegance of expression are natural for the poetry of a language in its infancy: we saw that Khari Boli Hindi as a literary medium was taking its first steps at the beginning of the 20th century, struggling to establish an adequate modern idiom and standard grammar, to find metres which would fit its natural rhythm.

Let us take as an example the verse above from *Bhārat-bhāratī*. Though we may not consider it great poetry, it demonstrates the care with which the poets of the Dwivedi period approached prosody. If we analyse its metrical structure we shall see that every line has a strict metrical pattern of 11+17 *mātrās* (the basic metrical instant which has the length of a short syllable). Each stanza consistently follows an AABB rhyme scheme. The problem with prosody in the Dwivedi period is not the lack of attention given to it, but the scarcity of indigenous poetic models to follow (the only readily available one was that of folk poetry in the Hindi area). Because of the absence of poetic tradition in Khari Boli Hindi, poets started by imitating Braj,[6] and later Sanskrit, Urdu, Bengali and English models, which, of course, did not fit the natural rhythm of Hindi. Moreover, they sometimes forced poets to subjugate meaning to metre.

Bhārat-bhāratī also demonstrates another characteristic of the poetry of the Dwivedi *yug*: it is social—it describes groups and collectivities rather than individuals. It is sufficient just to examine the subtitles of the *Vartamān khanda*, 'Book of the Present', of *Bhārat-bhāratī* to see this tendency towards typification: *Sādhusant* 'Sages and saints', *Brāhman* 'Brahmans', *Santān* 'Children', *Striyā* 'Women', etc. It is only from the Dwivedi *yug*'s successor, Hindi Neoromanticism (*Chāyāvād*), onwards that the reader will witness the plight of a woman, a widow, or beggar, portrayed as flesh-and-blood individuals rather than as social types.

Chāyāvād began in the early 1920s, historically a troubled time. It was the period between the two World Wars, a time of economic depression and unemployment; a time when an epidemic of influenza claimed thousands of lives. Perhaps most importantly for India, it was the time when, thanks to Gandhi, the national movement took a new turn. Whereas in the Dwivedi *yug* poetry was at one with its social and political circumstances, in *Chāyāvād* it was alienated from its immediate situation. Poets hid from social reality and instead inhabited a cosmic realm, an idealised world of intense beauty, mystical love and profound harmony. However, on another level *Chāyāvād* reflected the spirit of its time: the desire for political independence was translated in *Chāyāvād* into a quest for individual freedom.

Chāyāvād was the first movement in Hindi literature to shift the focus onto the individual experience and personal emotions.[7] This Indian version of Romanticism was an aesthetic, profoundly subjective movement, 'a cry of the heart against the strait-jacket of tradition' (Agyeya 1959, p.85). The individual, perceived to possess the grandeur and awesomeness of God, became the centre of this universe, the template for the description of any phenomenon: thus the two main subjects of *Chāyāvād*–nature and cultural tradition–were approached from a humanist perspective. For the first time tradition was reclaimed not as a public patriotic statement, but in a personally meaningful way. The focus on the individual also changed the poet's position. The stress shifted from the impact on the audience to the writer's intention; literary sensibility opened up to the values of subjectivity and originality. The poet's individual experience was expressed in a language which had ceased to be functional, but had instead become beautiful.

The innovation in content and form, the exploitation of 'the realm of the supernatural' and of 'the long ago' (Abrams 1988, p.115), the stress on the poet's own feelings, the sensuous description of the landscape are all features which *Chāyāvād* shares with its Western counterparts.[8] By the time *Chāyāvād*, emerged, English Romantic poetry, and especially the works of Wordsworth and Shelley, had become accessible to the intellectual elite in Hindi-speaking areas, partly directly and partly through the poetry of Tagore. However, *Chāyāvād* was nourished not only by this 'civilizational dialogue',[9] but also by a dialogue with Indian literary and philosophical tradition, both classical and medieval.

Let us enter a typical *Chāyāvādī* landscape through an extract of Pant's 'Almore kā vasant', 'Almora Spring'[10]–a magnificent picture of the splendour of nature awakening to a new life:

विद्रुम औ' मरकत की छाया,
सोने चाँदि का सूर्योतयः
हिम परिमल की रेशमी वायु,
शत रत्नछाय खग चित्रित नभ !
पतझड के कृश, पीले तन पर
पल्लवित तरूण लावन्य लोक :
शीतल हरितिमा की ज्वाला
फैलि दिशि दिशि कोमलाऽलोक !
(Pant 1966, p.73)

Coral and emerald shade
sun's heat first gold then silver;
snow mountain scent on silken breezes,
a hundred jeweled birds painting the sky.
On autumn's brittle yellow bodies
a world of new-born beauty budding,
while blaze of coolest green
sheds everywhere its tender light.
(Rubin 1993, p.136)

The striking originality of the imagery, the exquisiteness and refinement of the language, have no match in Dwivedi-*yug* poetry. We are first struck by the melodious diction, achieved by the preponderance of soft sounds, especially the liquid consonants *r* and *l*, the semivowel *y* and the sibilants *s* and *s*́ and the avoidance of harsh retroflex sounds. The vocabulary is Sanskritized: *sūrya*, *vāyu, sat, khag, nabh*, etc. are preferred to their Hindi counterparts. There is a lavish use of adjectives, to the almost total exclusion of verbs (unlike Dwivedi-*yug* poetry, where even the clumsy auxiliary verb is very common). The metrical structure is regular—there are 16 *mātrās* per line, but this regularity is not rigid and certainly not detrimental to meaning. The tendency to de-emphasise formal prosody is shown also by the preference for near-rhymes (*chāyā-vāyu*) instead of full rhymes.

However, this language of elegance and elusiveness was as detached from the coarse but buoyant speech of everyday life as the *Chāyāvādī* universe of beauty, harmony and love was from the reality of life in India in the '20s and 30s' of the 20th century. *Chāyāvād* set out to save Poetry from the dungeon of the Dwivedi *yug*: from its didacticism, puritanism, objectivity and linguistic philistinism, but instead locked her in the ivory tower of romantic subject matter and inaccessible idiom.

Pragativād, Progressivism, undertook the task of liberating poetry, of giving it forward motion, *pra-gati*. It brought poetry back into the world of social reality and gave it the idiom of common speech. In its early days *Pragativād* attempted to broaden the social sympathies of the writer and enhance the appeal and significance of literature, but soon the social was completely overtaken by the political, the individual by a social type. The time was ripe for proletarianism. The world economic crisis was felt also in India. The Communist Party of India was founded in 1925, and 1931 brought the first Hindi translation of the *Communist Manifesto*. The first conference of the pan-Indian[11] Progressive Writers' Association was held in 1936. Furthermore, 'by this time Gandhi had handed over the reins of the national movement to . . . Jawaharlal Nehru who in the 1920s had shown marked sympathy for socialism.' (Offredi 2001, pp.3–4) The 1936 conference of the Progressive Writers' Association was in effect the beginning of *Pragativād*; it declined as a movement in the 1950s, though some of the writers associated with it continued to write until the1980s.

KedarnathAgrawal's '*Karorō kā gānā*, 'The song of millions', is composed in the typical *Pragativādī* tone:

हरेक तार साँस का बजाये चल,
    बजाये चल, बजाये चल, बजाये चल।
हज़ारों आदमी का दल
हज़ारों औरतों का दल
तड़प-तड़प के है विकल:
नवीन जोश ज़िन्दगी जगाये चल,
    जगाये चल, जगाये चल, जगाये चल! ...
सभी का तन ग़ुलाम है,
सभी का मन ग़ुलाम है,

सभी की मति गुलाम है,
सभी की गति गुलाम है,
गुलामियों के चिन्ह को मिटाये चल !
    मिटाये चल, मिटाये चल, मिटाये चल !...
गगन में बिजलियाँ चलें
पवन में बिजलियाँ चलें
लहर में बिजलियाँ चलें
अजेय आत्मा का बल दिखाये चल,
    दिखाये चल, दिखाये चल, दिखाये चल !...
(Agrawal 1978, pp.68–9)

Playing each string of your breath, go,
    playing, go, playing, go, playing, go!
The army of thousands of men,
the army of thousands of women
is agitated and restless;
Awakening a new life-zeal, go,
    awakening, go, awakening, go, awakening, go!. . .
Everyone's body is enslaved,
everyone's mind is enslaved,
everyone's reason is enslaved,
everyone's movement is enslaved,
erasing the signs of slavery, go,
    erasing, go, erasing, go, erasing, go!. . .
Let lightning come in the sky,
let lightning come in the air,
let lightning come in the wave,
let lightning come on the path,
showing the strength of invincible soul, go,
    showing, go, showing, go, showing, go!. . .

This extract has all the qualities of a march: simplicity of both lexis and rhyme scheme, profusion of repetitions', short lines with a regular meter (except for the refrains) to support the marchers' measured tread. The idiom is clearly Marxist: the 'army' of 'enslaved' 'millions', the 'lightning' of revolution.

Thus the socialist realism of *Pragativād* replaced *Chāyāvād*'s world of dream and the individual was substituted by social types. Most of the progressive writers were of middle class urban origin; quite frequently they were completely ignorant of the mindsets and modes of living of the socially downtrodden they felt obliged to depict. Poetry regressed again to 'versified propaganda', filled with the oppressed, their oppressors and a revolution which was to bring about the 'Golden Dawn In Which The Worker Will Come Into His Own' (Agyeya 1959, p.95).

The spirit of rebellion was then born again and a new movement entered the literary scene: this was *Prayogvād*, 'Experimentalism' the infant who was to grow into *Nayī Kavitā*, the Hindi , 'incarnation' of New Poetry. *Prayogvād* was heralded by the publication in 1943 of a slim volume of poems called *Tār saptak*[12] which gave voice to seven young poets whose work had not been published· before. The anthology was edited by the poet and literary critic Agyeya, who through it and later publications became the chief theoretician of modernity in Hindi poetry. The importance of *Tār saptak* for the development of Hindi verse cannot be overstated–it was the herald of modernity in Hindi poetry. In the words of the German academic and translator Lothar Lutze, '1943 was the birth of Hindi literariness (Literaturetum)', '*Prayogvād* was the first purely literary movement in Hindi poetry'. (Lutze 1968, p.83)

In his introduction to *Tār saptak* Agyeya proclaimed that 'the poets included see poetry as a sphere of experiment. . . [they] do not claim that they have found the truth of poetry, but consider themselves to be mere seekers.' (Agyeya 1996a, p.9) 'They do not belong to any school, they have not reached any destination, they are still travellers–not even travellers, but seekers of a path. There is no ideological unity among them, their opinions on all important subjects–life, society, religion, poetic content and style, metre, the poet's responsibility–are different.' (ibid., p.10) Thus Agyeya proclaimed the first important characteristic of this new movement–unlike its predecessors it was not going to serve any particular agenda, any 'ism' (*vād*). Among the poets included in *Tār saptak* were Marxists like Muktibodh and Freudians like Agyeya, but as long as they continued to be 'seekers of a path' they were welcomed.

Tār saptak attracted much attention and the emerging movement was given the pejorative label[13] *Prayogvād* (Experimentalism) because of the frequency of the word *prayog* (experiment) in Agyeya's introduction. In his foreword to *Tār saptak*'s sequel *Dūsrā saptak* (The second heptad),[14] published in 1951, Agyeya engaged in a polemic with this name. 'Experiment is not an ideology (*vād*). We are not ideologists (*vādī*). Nor is experiment an aim or a goal. In the same way poetry has no ideology, poetry too is not an aim or a goal. Therefore it is as meaningful or meaningless to call us 'experimentalists' (*prayogvādī*) as it is to call us 'poetists' (*kavitāvādī*).' (Agyeya 1996b, p.6) Further on in the same introduction Agyeya elaborated on his interpretation of the term 'experiment': ·'Experiment is by itself not an aim, it is a means. . . It can help the poet to find out his/her truth and to express it better. Experiment can be applied to both the content and the form of a poetic work.' (ibid., pp.6–7). So Experimentalism set out to 'experiment' with both the content and form of poetry, or, if we follow the shift of terminology which happened around the publication of *Dūsrā saptak*, 'New poetry' set out to be 'new' in terms of both content and form.'[15] Let us examine more closely this 'newness'.

First we have to note a major shift of sensibility—in the words of Agyeya:
'during the inter-War period a. . . profound change had been developing. It was
not purely subjective, like Chhayavada, not merely objective-correlative, like
Pragativada, but a basic reorientation towards man. It was a growing awareness
of the unique total entity of man, of the integrity of the human individual.'
(Agyeya 1959, p.93) This 'quest for personality' (ibid.) in Hindi poetry was
undoubtedly influenced by Western Modernism, particularly by the poetry of
T.S. Eliot and Ezra Pound.[16] However, more to the point, it was brought about
by the human condition in a modern, urbanised, materialistic, technological
civillsation, by 'the sense of grief and apprehension with which the thinking
and feeling human being must record the loss of certainty, his awareness of the
efforts that he must make toward a comprehension of his disjointed world'
(Lange 1964, p.xiv).

The narrowing down of this universal experience of the world of modernity
in which 'all that is solid melts into air' [17] to the Indian conditions is perhaps
best formulated by Satchidanandan—modernity meant for India coping with:

> [t]he tensions bred by colonial education, the transformation of both
> Gandhism and Marxism, once ideologies of resistance, into formal
> establishment in the fifties, the loss of faith in every collective ideology,
> including religion, scepticism about the very idea of progress in the
> background of a half-hearted industrialisation that promoted economic
> inequality, impoverished rural life and gave rise to urban infernos with
> their faceless crowds, the growing disenchantment with the new polity
> and the erosion of values especially in the upper echelons of society,
> combined with the startling discoveries about the human unconscious,
> the novel perceptions of space and time.
>
> (Satchidanandan 2000, p.xxv)

These were the conditions, uncertainties, novelties with which the ordinary
man had to wrestle, and poetry became a witness to that match. The 'Hero' of
previous ages exited the scene now the writer focused not on constructing but
on discovering man (cf. Agyeya 1959, p.94). 'The despair or pessimism of the
late romantics and the forced optimism of Pragativada. . . [were] replaced by a
sober faith in man, which recognised his limitations and littleness' (ibid.,
p.95). The 'little man' (laghu mānav) came into the limelight. Every moment of
his existence became significant. Poetry expanded its subject matter to embrace
the ordinary man's life in its entirety. If we examine the poems included in the
following selection, we will see that wonderment at everyday life, the ironies
of daily existence, communion with nature, musings over philosophical issues,
the experience of the creative process, spirituality, love,

शिशिर का भोर	Dawn in winter
उत्ना-सा प्रकाश	Just enough light
कि अँधेरा दीखने लगे,	for darkness to show.
उत्नी-सी वर्षा	Just enough rain
कि सन्नाटा सुनाई दे जाये:	for silence to sound.
उत्ना- सा दर्द कि याद आये	Just enough pain to remember
कि भूल गया हूँ,	that I have forgotten,
भल गया हूँ . .	I have forgotten. . .

anguish, alienation, social inequality, patriarchal oppression, etc. etc. are all colours in the palette *of Nayī Kavitā*. On its canvas the bold strokes of the big questions of human existence merge with the nuances of its minutiae. Though *Nayī Kavitā* rejects progressivism as an ideology, it is enough to read Raghuvir Sahay or Kedarnath Singh in order to immediately notice the progressive background of the movement; however, 'progressive' is used here in its most general sense, as a translation *of pragatiśī*, rather than *pragativādī*.

A new poetics was required to express this 'continuing complexification of experience' (Satchidanandan 2000, p.xxv); the 'new' poets searched for new means of expression and for an articulate, accessible idiom. The experimentation with form led *Nayī Kavitā* to free verse, prevalent in European and American modern poetry. Metre was perceived as a possible obstruction to the flow of the poem; rhyme and regular verse were replaced by rhythm as an organising principle. *Lay* (rhythm) became a multi-layered concept, embracing not only the sound but also its meaning.[18]

It is important to be aware that the rejection of traditional metres and stanza patterns and the embracing of free verse does not mean technical laxness. Let us take one of Agyeya's poems included in this anthology as a proof for the extreme care given to poetic form.

This poem consists of three propositions structured in the same way: a verbless phrase, including the diminutive form of the adjective *utnā* 'as much' and the nouns 'light', 'rain' and 'pain', followed by a clause, made of the nouns 'darkness', 'silence' and 'memory' and a subjunctive verb. This parallelism links natural and human—light, rain and pain. However, there is an important difference between the first two propositions and the last one, and it is precisely this variation which brings about the intense painfulness of the poem: the natural phenomena are presented in dichotomies—light-darkness, (the sound of) rain-silence—which interact, with the paradoxical consequence that darkness and silence are resolved, lose their identity, become visible and audible. The human emotion, though, is not counterbalanced by its opposite; unlike light and rain, it is linked in a three-component chain of pain-memory-oblivion in which the opposition is between the last two: they can interact and be resolved, but the pain will stay. Thus we see how the extremely tight structure of this poem enhances its meaning.

The innovations of form in *Nayī Kavitā* embrace not only prosody, but also poetic vocabulary. Vivid contemporary speech was chosen as the vehicle of *Nayī Kavitā*. The experimentation with language opened poetry's gates to lexis from different sources: the 'high style' of Sanskrit; Perso-Arabic, common in colloquial Hindi, but previously excluded from its poetry and even English. *Nayī Kavitā's*, 'rage to order words'[19] evokes Gottfried Benn's image of the poet functioning 'in a laboratory of words' where 'he models, manufactures words, opens them, explodes them, smashes them, in order to charge them with tensions that will continue for several decades.' (Lange 1964, p.xxii)

Despite this emphasis on form, in the best examples of *Nayī Kavitā* experimentation with form is never self-serving. In his introduction to *Tīsrā saptak* (The third heptad), published in 1959, Agyeya differentiates *Nayī Kavitā* from the contemporaneous formalist movement of *Nakenvād*[20] which indulges in a cult of the Word, where experiment becomes the ultimate goal, rather than a means to express new content (cf. Agyeya 1996c, pp.6–7).

Probably this is enough basic signposting to ensure that the traveller on the path of Hindi poetry does not get lost in the *Nayī Kavitā* zone, to which this book is dedicated. But where does this zone finish? The answer to this question will depend on our interpretation of the term *Nayī Kavitā*. Seen as a particular literary movement with its organs and manifestos it probably ended in the second half of the 1960s, when its main platform–the journal *Nayī Kavitā*[21]–ceased to be published. In the 1960s *Nayī Kavitā* co-existed with 'movements' like *Sanātan Sūryodayī Kavitā* (Eternal Sunrise Poetry), *Yuyutsāvādī Kavitā* (Bellicose Poetry), *Asvīkrt Kavitā* (Unaccepted Poetry), *Akavitā* (Non-Poetry), *Bhīt Kavitā* [sic] (Beat Poetry), *Tāzī Kavitā* (Fresh Poetry), *Pratibaddh Kavitā* (Committed Poetry) and *Sahaj Kavitā* (Natural Poetry) (cf. Gaeffke 1978, p.92). The very length of this list (which does not claim to be comprehensive) suggests the absurdity of seeing all these developments as totally separate movements.[22] This is why I prefer to interpret *Nayī Kavitā* as a general modernist tendency which insists on depicting 'the present in its presentness';[23] in this sense *Nayī Kavitā* is very much alive in contemporary Hindi poetry.

This interpretation of *Nayī Kavitā* informs my choice of poems included in this book. It is true that all the male poets I have selected first published their work in one of the *Saptaks*: Muktibodh and Agyeya in *Tār saptak*; Shamsher Bahadur Singh and Raghuvir Sahay in *Dūsrā saptak*; Sarveshwar Dayal Saksena, Kunwar Narain and Kedarnath Singh in *Tīsrā saptak*. However, I have not limited my choice to poems written at the time when *Nayī Kavitā* was flourishing as a movement; all the poets included in this book continued writing later as well, and some of them, like Kunwar Narain and Kedarnath Singh, are still active. My representation of each poet's works is based on as much of his/her oeuvre as I could find; often my preferences have been for later, more mature poems, though in order to give some sense of the evolution of the poet I have tried to not completely ignore earlier work.

As Ramakrishnan points out in his introduction to *Tree of tongues*, 'every anthology tells a story of its own—a story of omissions and exclusions, likes and dislikes, receptions and rejections' (Ramakrishnan 1999, p.xix). This book is no exception. My selection is subjective and does not claim to be comprehensive. In my choice of poems I have been guided by several considerations: that the poem should speak to me, that the language of the original should not present an insurmountable obstacle to a non-native speaker of Hindi, that its length should preferably comply with the space restrictions in a book of this kind, and that the poems should reflect the thematic richness of their authors' oeuvre. I have tried to include (at least extracts of) poems which have attracted much critical attention and become 'classics' of contemporary Hindi poetry—works like Muktibodh's 'Ādhere mẽ' or Agyeya's 'Asādhya vīnā'. But I have also been careful to not just repeat the selections in other anthologies, and to avoid poems which have been translated many times. In my translations I have followed the original as closely as possible in order to assist readers who may want to read the translations in conjunction with the originals. However, I have tried not to allow literalness to kill the poetic. This is a balancing act, as all who translate poetry know.

My choice of male voices is very orthodox—I have put together my own 'Saptak' of writers who have already secured their place in the canon of Hindi poetry. I have done this on purpose, for this anthology is meant as an introduction to the landscape of Hindi verse and so should present some of its highest peaks. However, I have also taken the 'opportunity to revise the literary map' (Mehrotra 1992, p.8), an editor's privilege, by readdressing the balance somewhat between male and female writing. All anthologies of contemporary Hindi poetry have followed Agyeya's model of male dominance: only two women—Kirti Chaudhury and Shakunt Mathur—rub shoulders with the nineteen male poets included in his three famous *Saptaks*. Unsurprisingly, therefore, the literary critic Ramvilas Sharma believes that 'in the entire *Nayī Kavitā* movement there are no women poets to be mentioned' (G. Singh 2000, p.3). My search through the journal *Nayī Kavitā* and magazines like *Kalpanā* proved this statement wrong: I managed to locate works by about twenty women poets. However most of them have sunk into oblivion: no collections of their verses have been published, no secondary material has been written on them; apart from a few poems which were allowed to become public, these poets remain silent or perhaps even silenced.

We can speculate at length about the forces which sentenced these women to silence (indeed I have done so in my article 'Shakespeare's sister in India: In search of Hindi women poets', Rosenstein 2001). No doubt patriarchy has deprived women of adequate education and exposure to the vastness of human experience, belief in their own creativity, financial independence and an opportunity for self-realisation outside the enclosures of domesticity. It has been difficult for women to break into a male-dominated literary establishment. It is not by chance that the three women poets of the *Nayī Kavitā* (and post-*Nayī Kavitā*) generation who have gained some recognition–Shakunt Mathur, Kirti Chaudhury and Jyotsna Milan–come from and/or have married into families of literati.

I have chosen to include in this selection four women poets–Shakunt Mathur, Kanta, Amrita Bharati, and Jyotsna Milan–hoping to present a more balanced picture *of Nayī Kavitā*. I must quickly add that these poets have their significance as practitioners of the art of poetry, regardless of their sex. My choice here may seem strange: why have I excluded Kirti Chaudhury, who after all was allowed into the third *Saptak*? Conversely, why have I included Jyotsna Milan, who is strictly speaking not of the *Nayī Kavitā* generation?

Let me try to' pre-empt these criticisms. I chose not to include Kirti Chaudhury because of the shortness of her poetic career. My reason for connecting Jyotsna Milan with *Nayī Kavitā* is that she did publish in its organ, even if it is true that most of her poetry was written after the end of the movement.

On a more general level I could be accused of giving voice to women poets while silencing the popular lyricists–who have been as ignored by elitist critics as have the women poets by the male-dominated literary establishment. After all, modern poetry in Hindi rests on a huge bed of popular poetry. Poets like Bachchan or Suman, and lyricists of the 'Hindi' film like Javed Akhtar draw huge audiences, but remain invisible to the elitist critic. I have to plead guilty to this charge; my guilt is mitigated by my awareness of the necessary limitations of a book of this kind. Perhaps this anthology will inspire somebody to do for popular Hindi verse what I have tried to do for *Nayī Kavitā*.

Agyeya reminds editors that 'the role of an introduction is to prepare the ground; the ground is 'ready' when one can walk on it without anxiety and forget about it. Now is time for the reader to walk on and meet the poets.' (Agyeya 1996c, p.11)

Notes and References

1 Modern Hindi, also called Khari Boli, is 'the present-day language of government, education, literature and public life in the central states of North India, and the official national language of India. A more Sanskritised form of the colloquial "Hindustani" lingua franca, it has been evolving since the early nineteenth century and is presently the dominant literary language for the whole Hindi area'. (Schomer 1983, p.1)

2   The term 'Medieval Hindi' is perhaps misleading, because it suggests that the dialects to which it refers are inherently medieval. However, it is a common label for a range of related dialects which developed in the Hindi speaking area from the eleventh century onwards. The following description of the Medieval Hindi dialects is based on Schomer 1983, pp.1–4.

3   I have used R.S. McGregor's translation of the title of this poem, see McGregor' 1974, p.109. All English translations are mine unless stated otherwise.

4   *Bhārat-bhāratī* is a long poem (184 pages in the 1920 edition) which consists of three parts: 'Book of the past', 'Book of the present' and 'Book of the future'; all three are divided into numerous sub-sections.

5   The Arya Samaj was founded in 1875 by Swami Dayananda Saraswati. It was a religious and social reform movement whose goal was to purify Hinduism by returning to the religion and society of the ancient scriptures, the Vedas. It rejected caste restrictions, child marriage, the ban on the remarriage of widows, as well as image worship and the mythology of divine incarnations.

6   Just to get a taste of how different Braj is from its successor, Khari Boli Hindi, in terms of vocabulary, grammar, melody and prosody, let us look at a couplet by the 17th-century poet Vrinda:

आडंबर तजि किजिए गुन संग्रह चित चाय।

छीर रहित गड ना बिकै, आनिय घट बँधाय॥

'Abandoning ostentation, accumulate pleasing qualities;

a milkless cow will not be sold by tying a bell to it.'

(Snell 1991, pp.160, 161)

This couplet is in one of the most common metres of medieval Hindi poetry–*dohā*–each of the two lines consists of 24 *mātrās* in the arrangement 6+4+3, 6+4+1. Vrinda's poetic mastery is evident from the aptness of the illustration given in the second line of the contention of the first line and from his skilful use of sound patterns: assonance and alliteration.

7   For a very interesting discussion of this shift of sensibilities see Rubin 1993, pp.1–26.

8   For a description of the characteristics of the English Romanticism cf. Abrams 1988, pp.115–16.

9   This is a term used by Satchidanandan 2000, p.xxviii.

10 Pant, one of the four major *Chāyāvādī* poets, grew up at the village of Kasauni and the nearby town of Almora, and the magnificent landscape of the Himalayan foothills remained a constant source of inspiration throughout his career.

11 Not only *Pragativād*, but most movements on the Hindi literary scene had their parallels in other Indian languages. As Dharwadker points out, between 1900 and 1930 'various Indian languages collectively went through a phase of intensely nationalist writing'; 'between about 1920 and 1935, the Indian languages passed through a new nation-wide phase of "Romantic" writing'; 'two. . . simultaneous national movements appeared in the 1930s': the Progressive movement and the 'Indian counterpart of Anglo-American modernism, in which poets in practically every language broke away from traditional metres, stanza patterns, styles, materials, and themes to invent "free verse" poetry.' (Dharwadker 1996, pp.187–9).

12 *Tār saptak* means 'upper octave' and refers to the highest of three octaves that make the ideal range of human voice in Indian music. The musical analogy is complicated by the fact that what the Western tradition sees as a sequence of eight

notes is seen in the Indian tradition as a series of intervals between the notes, and therefore achieves a total of only seven. (I owe this reference to Rupert Snell.) This is why there are seven poets in *Tār saptak; saptak* by itself means a 'heptad'.

[13] In the same way as *Chāyāvād* attracted criticism from the champions of both Braj poetry and Dwivedi *yug* verse, because of its radically new poetic sensibility, and was given the originally disparaging label *Chāyāvād* (shadowism), suggesting that this poetry was vague and insubstantial, *Tār saptak* poetry was labelled *Prayogvād* by some progressive critics who claimed that it was formalist and decadent. (cf. Kumar 1988, p.16)

[14] It appears that in *Dūsrā* and *Tīsrā saptak* Agyeya abandoned the musical analogy —the logical progression down the scale to *madhya* (medium) and *mandra* (low) octaves. However, it is significant that the original title seems to have anticipated a sequence of three (but no more) *saptaks*. In fact a *Cauthā saptak* (Fourth heptad) was published in 1979, but unlike its predecessors, it left no mark on the development of Hindi poetry.

[15] However, this does not mean that *Nayī Kavitā* turned its back on tradition. It was not tradition but its blind imitation that *Nayī Kavitā* rejected. In Agyeya's words: 'tradition is not a bundle which the poet can put on his head and walk off. Tradition has no meaning for the poet until he closely scrutinises it, tears it to shreds to examine it and appropriates it.' (Agyeya 1966b, p.6)

[16] 'Indian poets were fascinated by Eliot's criticism of contemporary civilisation, its spiritual emptiness, decay, nihilism and loneliness. In his work they found the means of expression suitable for their own spirituality (such as irony and sneering melancholy). In Pound's poetry they discovered innovatory language, conciseness, discipline of phrase and rhythm, intellectual ingeniousness, condensed imagery and erudition' (Czekalska 1999, p.3). For the influence of English poetry on modern Hindi poetry see also Varma 1980 and Narain 1998, pp.103–10.

[17] Marx, quoted in Berman 1993, p.15.

[18] J. Gupta wrote a detailed discussion of *artha kī lay* (the rhythm of meaning) in which he followed Eliot's and Richards's ideas about the symbiosis of meaning and rhythm (See Gupta 1956). The following passage from Richards, quoted by Gupta, summarises this concept: 'the rhythm which we admire, which we seem to detect actually *in* the sounds, and which we seem to respond to, is something which we only *ascribe* to them and is, actually, a rhythm of the mental activity through which we apprehend not only the sound of the words but their sense'. (Richards 1991, p.229)

[19] This is a phrase used by Victor Lange in his 'Introduction' to *Contemporary German poetry*, Lange 1964, p.xxii.

[20] *Naken* is an acronym of the first names of the three poets who started the movement: Nalin Vilochan Sharma, Kesari Kumar and Naresh.

[21] Eight issues of *Nayī Kavitā* were published between 1954 and 1967 under the editorship of Jagdish Gupta. After 1967 the journal ceased to exist.

[22] A similar explosion of 'movements' after *Nayī Kahānī* (New story), which as its name suggests is the parallel in fiction of *Nayī Kavitā*, happens also in the Hindi short story. There too the rapid proliferation of 'movements' suggests fashion and fight for recognition rather than totally different developments (cf. Rosenstein 1993, pp.117–31)

[23] Baudelaire quoted in Calinescu 1987, p.49.

AGYEYA

(Sachchidananda Hirananda Vatsyayan) 1911–1987

The pen-name which the writer Jainendra Kumar accidentally gave to Sachchidananda Hirananda Vatsyayan summarises the difficulties faced by scholars who try to study him: he is *agyeya (ajñeya* in a strict transliteration), 'unknowable'. It is not lack of data that makes it so hard to grasp the essence of this towering personality; indeed a meticulous biographer could spend years ploughing through countless books on Agyeya and his creative writings, through interviews with him, and through his diaries and other works. And yet Agyeya remains unknowable, a 'handsome masked man' in the words of Krishna Baldev Vaid, 'a mysterious summit', *rahasyamay śekhar* (Machwe 1991, p.6)–a prototype of his famous character Shekhar.

His personae were manifold: the poet Agyeya and the literary critic Sachchidananda Vatsyayan, the keen explorer of Western culture and the devotee of 'Indianness', the terrorist and the humanist, the soldier and the writer, the solitary man and the public figure; all his life he showed different facets of his personality to different people in different ways. The loneliness of his early years (because of his father's belief in traditional education and constant transfers he never went to school) and the solitary cell in Delhi jail to which he was confined between 1931 and 1934 taught him the habit of solitude; writing became his means of communicating.

It is difficult to encapsulate the essence of Agyeya not only because of this cocoon of solitude, which he vehemently defended, but also because of the sheer volume of his endeavours. Reading through a description of his various pursuits is a humbling and tiring experience: an anti-British revolutionary between 1929 and 1934 who used his training in science to produce bombs; a soldier in World War II between 1943 and 1946; an editor on various Hindi and English magazines (starting as a child in the family journal *Ānanda Bandhu* and proceeding to *Sainik, Visāl Bhārat, Pratīk, Dinmān, Nayā Pratīk, Everyman's*) and All India Radio throughout his life; a lecturer in universities in India and abroad (Jodhpur, California, Berkeley, Chicago, Bonn and Heidelberg); a translator from English, Hindi and Bengali; a writer of fourteen collections of poems, six books of short stories, four novels, twenty volumes of essays, a play, two travelogues, three diaries; an editor of various publications; a restless traveller to countless destinations in India, Europe, Australia, America, Japan, Vietnam and the Philippines.

The list of subjects Agyeya had mastered, the practical skills he possessed, and hobbies he was devoted to is no shorter and suggests a rare combination of deft hands and encyclopaedic intellect: he was a gifted linguist–competent in Punjabi, Hindi, Urdu, Sanskrit, Bengali, Gujarati, Tamil, English, French and German; a scholar of art, music, dance, drama, photography, film-making, archaeology and astrology; an expert in gardening, carpentry, tailoring and mechanics; a dexterous driver of all sorts of vehicles (including helicopters); and an experienced mountaineer.

Agyeya's contemporaries describe him as an attractive man, 'the rajah of the revolutionary movement'–standing out with his handsome, noble features– as a man of strong opinions and intolerance, of an explosive, stormy temperament. He inherited his father's cult of the traditional Brahmanical virtues of sacrifice, fearlessness and truth–it was not by chance that his childhood name was *Sacca* (true, truthful). His writing and his life are permeated with a sense of restlessness, of an unsettled spirit on an endless journey in search of a non-existent home. This homelessness is reflected in the name of his last collection *Aisā koī ghar apne dekhā hai?* (Have you seen such a home?) and in his fanciful idea of building himself a home in the branches of a tree.

Agyeya's writing has pushed back boundaries in big, difficult, passionate subjects: the nature of the creative process, tradition and modernity, social and ethical questions, death and freedom, love and war, language and silence. It is far beyond the scope of this introduction to try to summarise them all, but highlighting some may enhance an understanding of his poetry. Despite his active political life, Agyeya is a firm believer in the autonomy of literature: art which serves politics is no art. Trained as a scientist, he is nevertheless weary of gigantic cities and the Western cult of technology and materialism. Notwithstanding his exposure to and interest in Western culture, he considers himself a devotee of Indian civilisation. Like his contemporaries abroad, his works reflect the individual's search for values in a world deprived of a traditional basis for values. He responds to time as a moment *(ksan)*, not as a flow. Influenced by Zen Buddhism, some of his best lyrics are mystic experiences of 'pure' moments. Agyeya worships silence: it is the quality which gives majestic dignity to some of the characters in his novels; it is the essence of poetry–'the poetry is not in language, it is not even in the words: it is in the silence between words. And the poet knows intuitively that *the other* can be reached and dialogue established because he knows that communication is possible through silence' (quoted in Das 1990, p.148).

As the poems below suggest, most of Agyeya's lyrics are meditations on Nature, the Divine and Man, reflections of eternity in the moment, reminiscent of Rolland's '"oceanic" feeling of something limitless, unbounded' (quoted in Storr 1988, p.37). Love and memory, the creative process and history, dream and reality are some of Agyeya's favourite topics. He does not turn a blind eye to the problems of everyday life either—quite a few of his poems are social satires.

In an interview with Raghuvir Sahay (Lele, undated, p.30) Agyeya defines a great poet as somebody who has a large output, who develops throughout his life, who exerts significant influence over his contemporaries, and whose poetry stands the test of time. There is no Hindi poet in the second half of the twentieth century who fits this definition of greatness more closely than Agyeya.

The text of the poems is taken from Agyeya 1986; for other translations see Agyeya 1976 and 1981; Misra 1967, pp.56, 78, 92, 113 and 116; Dharwadker 1996, p.164; Vajpeyi 1998, pp.25–34; Satchidandan 2000, pp.34–8 and *Indian horizons*, vol. 42, pp.30–1. Interesting 'introductions' to Agyeya are Machwe 1991 and Misra 1990; Ray 1986 is a full-scale biography; Lele (undated) and Sharatkumar 1988 are transcripts of interviews with Agyeya.

Agyeya

दूर्वाचल

पार्श्व गिरि का नम्र, चीड़ों में
डगर चढ़ती उमंगों –सी ।
बिछी पैरों में नदी ज्यों दर्द की रेखा ।
विहग–शिशु मौन नीड़ों में
मैंने आँख भर देखा ।
दिया मन को दिलासा–पुन: आऊँगा ।
(भले ही बरस दिन–अनगिन युगों के बाद !)
क्षितिज ने पलक–सी खोली,
तमक कर दामिनी बोली –
'अरे यायावर, रहेगा याद ?'

Verdant hill

Mountainside, bowed; among the pines
a path, climbing, like rapture.
At my feet a river laid like the contour of pain.
Little birds, silent, in their nests.
I looked my fill
and consoled my heart–I will return
(even if after days, years–countless aeons!)
The horizon opened its eyelids,
a lightning flushed with anger:
'O wanderer, will you remember?'

उषा-दर्शन

मैं ने कहा, डूब, चाँद !
रात को सिहरने दे, कुइँयों को मरने दे,
आक्षितिज तम फैल जाने दे ।
– पर तम थमा और मुझ ही में जम गया ।
मैं ने कहा – उठ री लजीली भोर –रश्मि, सोयी
दुनिया में तुझे कोई देख मत, मेरे भीतर समा जा तू,
चुपके से मेरी यह हिमाहत नलिनी खिला जा तू ।
–वो प्रगल्भा मानमयी
बावली-सी उठ सारी दुनिया में फैल गयी !

Seeing dawn

I said, Moon, sink!
Let the night shiver, the lilies die,

darkness fill the horizon.
–But darkness stood still and gathered inside me.
I said, Bashful dawn-ray, rise, let
no one in the sleeping world see you, fill me,
quietly make my frost-nipped lily bloom.
–The conceited capricious lady,
frenzied, rose and filled the whole world!

रात में गाँव

झिंगुरों की लोरियाँ
सुला गयी थीं गांव को,
झोपडे हिंडोलों–सी झुला रही हैं
धीमे–धीमे
उजली कपासी धूम –डो रियाँ।

Village at night

The cicadas' lullabies
put the village to sleep,
smoke's bright cotton-white cords
are rocking the huts like cradles
gently.

चुप-चाप

चुप-चाप चुप-चाप
झरने का स्वर
हम में भर जाय,

चुप -चाप चुप-चाप
शरद की चॉदनी
झील की लहरों पर तिर आय,

चुप-चाप चुप-चाप
जीवन का रहस्य
जो कहा न जाय, हमारी
ठहरी आँखों में गहराय,

चुप-चाप चुप-चाप
हम पुलकित विराट् में डूबें
पर विराट् हम में मिल जाय –

चुप-चाप, चुप-चा ऽ ऽ प . . .

Quietly

Quietly
may the murmur of water falling
fill us,

quietly
may the autumn moon
float on the ripples of the lake,

quietly
may life's unspoken mystery
deepen in our still eyes,

quietly
may we, ecstatic, be immersed in the expanse
yet find it in ourselves—
quiet. . . ly. . .

शिशिर का भोर

उत्ना-सा प्रकाश
कि अँधेरा दीखने लगे,
उत्नी-सी वर्षा
कि सन्नाटा सुनाई दे जाये;
उत्ना-सा दर्द कि याद आये
कि भूल गया हूँ,
भूल गया हूँ . . .

Dawn in winter

Just enough light
for darkness to show.
Just enough rain
for silence to sound.
Just enough pain to remember
that I have forgotten,
I have forgotten . . .

नन्दा देवि १४

निचले
हर शिखर पर
देवल :
ऊपर
निराकार
तुम
केवल . . .

Nanda Devi 14[1]

Below
on every summit
a shrine
Above
formless you
alone . . .

असाध्य वीणा

सहसा वीणा झनझना उठी –
संगीतकार की आँखों में ठंडी पिघली ज्वाला-सी झलक गयी –
रोमांच एक बिजली-सा सबके तन में दौड़ गया।
अवतरित हुआ संगीत
स्वयंभू
जिस में सोता है अखण्ड
ब्रह्ग का मौन
अशेष प्रभामय।

डूब गये सब एक साथ।
सब अलग-अलग एकाकी पार तिर।

राजा ने अलग सुना :
जय देवि यशःकाय
वरमाल लिये
गाती थी मंगल-गीत,
दुन्दुभी दूर कहीं बजती थी,
राज-मुकुट सहसा हलका हो आया था, मानो हो फूल सिरिस का।
ईर्ष्या, महदाकांक्षा द्वेष, चाटुता
सभी पुराने लुगड़े-से झर गये, निखर आया था जीवन–
धर्म-भाव से जिसे निछावर वह कर देगा।

रानी ने अलग सुना :
छँटती बदली में एक कौंध कह गयी–
तुम्हारे ये मणि-माणक , कण्ठहार, पट-वस्त्र,
मेखला-किंकिणि–
सब अन्धकार के कण हैं ये! आलोक एक है
प्यार अनन्य! उसी की
विद्युल्लता घेरती रहती है रस-भार मेघ को,
थिरक उसी की छाती पर उस में छिप कर सो जाती है
आश्वस्त, सहज विश्वास-भरी ।
रानी
उस एक प्यार को साधेगी ।

सब ने भी अलग-अलग संगीत सुना ।
इस को

वह कृपा-वाक्य था प्रभुओं का।
उस को
आतंक-मुक्ति का आश्वासन !
इस को
वह भरी तिजोरी में सोने की खनक।
उसे
बटुली में बहुत दिनों के बाद अन्न की सौंधी खुशबू।
किसी एक को नयी वधू की सहमी-सी पायल-ध्वनि।
किसी दूसरे को शिशु की किलकारी।
एक किसी को जाल-फँसी मछली की तड़पन-
एक अपर को चहक मुक्त नभ में उड़ती चिड़िया की।
एक तीसरे को मण्डी की ठेलमठेल, गाहकों की आस्पर्धा-भरि बोलियाँ,
चौथे को मन्दिर की ताल-युक्त घण्टा-ध्वनि।
और पाँचवें को लोहे पर सधे हथौड़े को सम चोटें
और छठे को लंगर पर कसमसा रही नौका पर लहरों की अविराम थपक।
बटिया पर चमरौधे की रूँधी चाप सातवें के लिए-
और आठवें को कुलिया की कटी मेड़ से बहते जल की छुल-छुल।
इसे गमक नटिन की एड़ी के घुँघरू की।
उसे युद्ध का ढोल।
इसे संझा-गोधूली की लघु टुन-टुन –
उसे प्रलय का डमरू-नाद।
इस को जीवन की पहलि अँगड़ाई
पर उस को महाजृम्भ विकराल काल !
सब डूबे, तिरे, झिंपे, जागे –
हो रहे वशंवद, स्तब्धः
इयत्ता सब की अलग-अलग जागी,
संधीत हुई,
पा गयी विलय।
वीणा फिर मूक हो गयी।

The indomitable lute[2]

Suddenly the lute resounded–
A cold, liquid blaze flashed in the musician's eyes–
A thrill like lightning ran through each body.
Music descended,
self-born,
Brahma's[3] unbroken silence,
infinite, lustrous
sleeping in it.

All were immersed, together.
All were carried across, separate, alone.

The king only heard:
The goddess of victory, fame-bodied,
singing an auspicious hymn,
garland in hand;
drums resounded in the distance.

At once his crown grew light, like a mimosa–
Envy, great ambition, hatred, flattery
were all shed like old rags, and life's gold purified
for him to dutifully sacrifice.

The queen only heard
lightning say in the scattered cloud–
These jewels and gems of yours, these necklaces, garments,
girdles and bells
are mere fragments of darkness! Single-minded love alone
is light! Its
lightning entwines the cloud–pleasure amass–
she swings on his chest, rests on it,
assured, full of pure trust.
The queen will strive for such love.

All heard different music.
To this one
it was God's utterance of grace.
To that one
a promise of no more fear!
To this one
the jingle of gold in brim-full safe.
To that one
the delicious aroma of cooking after days of hunger!

To one the timid tinkle of a new bride's anklets
To another the joyful shouts of a child.
To someone the thrashing of a fish caught in a net–
To another the warbling of a bird, soaring in the infinite.
To one the jostling at a market, customers' scramble
To another the rhythmical chime of temple bells.
To one the steady blows of a hammer on an anvil,
To someone else the ceaseless tapping of waves on a boat that chafes at
    anchor.
To one footsteps, confined in clogs, on a village path
To another the gurgle of water streaming from a broken dyke.
To this one the tinkle of a dancing girl's anklets.
To that one the thunder of a battle.

To one the gentle chime of twilight–
To another the beat of doom's drums
To this one youth's langour
and to that one time's hideous yawn!
All immersed, sunk, drifted, roused–
subdued, dumbfounded:
Everyone's self awoke alone,
united,
merged.

The lute grew still once more.

जो पुल बनायेंगे

जो पुल बनायेंगे
वे अनिवार्यतः
पीछे रह जायेंगे ।
सेनाएँ हो जायेंगी पार
मारे जायेंगे रावण
जयी होंगे राम;
जो निर्माता रहे
 इतिहास में
बन्दर कहलायेंगे ।

The builders of bridges[4]

The builders of bridges
will inevitably
be left behind.
Armies will cross
Ravanas will be killed
Ramas will be victorious
In [the annals of] history
the builders
will be called monkeys.

काले मेग्दान

इधर
परकोटे और भीतरी दीवार के बीच
लम्बी खाई में
ढंग से सँवरे हुए
पिछले महायुद्ध के हथियारों के ढूह :
रुँडे टैंक , टुण्डी तोपें, नकचिपटे गोला-फेंक
सब की पपोटे-रहित अन्धी आँखें
ताक रहीं आकाश ।

उधर
परकोटे और दीवार के बीच टीले पर
बेढंगे झंखाड़ों से अधढँके
मठ और गिरजाघर के खँडहर
चौकाठ-रहित खिड़कियों से उमड़ता अँधियारा
मनुष्यों को मानो खोजता हो धरती पर ...
ईश्वर रे, मेरे बेचारे,
तेरे कौन रहे अधिक हत्यारे ?

Kalemegdan[5]

On this side
in a long moat
between the rampart and the inner wall
carefully ordered
stacks of weapons from the last war:
tank trunks, mutilated cannons, flat-nosed mortars–
their unblinking blind eyes
staring at the sky.

On that side
on a mound
between the rampart and the wall,
half overgrown by disorderly thickets
ruins of a monastery and a church
darkness surging from frameless windows
as if seeking men on the earth . . .
God, my poor God,
who murdered you more?

नरक की समस्या

नरक ? खैर और तो जो है सो है,
जैसे जिये, उस से वहाँ कोई खास कष्ट नहीं होगा ।
पर एक बात है : जिस से जिस से यहाँ बचना चाहा
वह-वह भी वहीं होंगा !

The problem with hell

Hell? Never mind, what's there is there.
It won't be much more wretched than life.
But the snag is: everybody I tried to escape here
will be there too!

Notes and References

1 This is the 14th poem of the 'Nanda Devi' cycle, Nanda Devi being a famous Himalayan peak. Nanda is also an epithet of the goddess Durga.

2 'Āsādhya vīnā' is one of Agyeya's longest (10 pages in the edition I have used) and most praised poems. It is said to be based on a Japanese folk tale; its narrative revolves around a lute which could never be mastered, and remained silent until, finally, an ascetic cajoled wondrous music out of it. The extract given here describes the reaction of the royal audience to the vīnā's magical sound. What makes this passage particularly interesting is the multitude of responses, reflecting the limitlessness of the universal form of the Supreme Being in which all Creation is manifest–the vastness of Creation. In this extract Agyeya also tackles the opposition between separateness (the recognition of identity) and merging (the surrender of the listeners' ego to the music). But it is not only the audience which surrenders to the music; the musician himself has to surrender to it, and to the instrument, for the creative act to take place. Thus 'Āsādhya vīnā' addresses a question central to Agyeya's artistic world–that of the philosophy of creativity. It depicts creation as a dynamic process, a merging of the artistic ego, surrender.

3 Brahma is regarded as Creator of the world. As such he is the first of the Hindu Trinity, alongside Vishnu, the Preserver, and Shiva, the Destroyer. Reduced to playing an active part only at the beginning of the world cycle, he is often thought of as sunk in cosmic slumber or deep meditation and has to be awakened when needed.

4 This poem is an example of Agyeya's creative reinterpretation of tradition. He uses the story of the Rāmāyana to meditate on history as an interplay of creation and destruction, on its attitude to leaders and ordinary men. The leaders, the victorious king Ram and the defeated demon Ravan, are remembered, but their battle would not have been possible had Hanuman's monkeys not built a bridge for Ram to cross the sea to Ravan's abode, the isle of Lanka. The builders of bridges, the humble creators, are 'left behind'. In the translation I have marked the inherent -a at the end of Ram's and Ravan's names for euphony.

5 Kalemegdan is the name of a fortress, situated at the confluence of the Danube and Sava, which has been turned into a museum.

My poetry is the expression of a restless mind looking for its path.[1]

Gajanan Madhav Muktibodh
1917–1964

In the summer of 1964, while Muktibodh lay in coma in a hospital bed, brought to the threshold of death by stroke and meningitis, his friends were preparing the publication of *Cā̃d kā mũh terhā hai* (The moon's face is crooked), his first collection of poems. He did not live to see his book. The sixteen poems he contributed to Agyeya's *Tār saptak* and about thirty verses published in different magazines (*Vāṇī, Karmvĩr Ārtī, Vīṇā, Vicār, Hams, Lok yuddha, Dharmayug, Lahar, Sārthī, Kavi,* etc.) were the only ones to appear in his lifetime. And yet, ever since his untimely death, his poetry has been in the limelight of Hindi literary discussion. As Ashok Vajpeyi points out, 'no responsible reader or contemporary critic can prove his authority without a link to Muktibodh' (Vajpeyi 1994, p.1). Superlatives pile against his name: he is compared with the giant of 20th-century Hindi verse, Nirala (Bandopadhyaya 1994, p.149); he is called 'the most original poet of *Tār saptak*' (Jain 1965, p.16); his *Cā̃d kā mũh terhā hai* has been labelled 'the highest achievement in modern Hindi poetry' (Gaeffke 1978, p.88).

What turned this relatively unknown, small-town poet into 'an event in the world of Hindi poetry' (Jain 1965, p.9)? Muktibodh's final tragic battle with death caught the public's attention and focused it on all the earlier struggles of his life, on his tortured existence and on his obscure poetry.

Muktibodh lived 'in debt and insecurity, in dingy dwellings in small towns of Madhya Pradesh' (Bandopadhyaya 1994, p.150). Born in Sheopur (Madhya Pradesh) in the family of a police inspector, his nomadic existence started quite early, following his father's transfers. After completing his BA in 1938, Muktibodh continued this life of wandering, moving from one town to the next in search of employment: he became a teacher in Ujjain, and again in Shujalpur, an editor of *Hams* in Benares, a teacher and journalist in Jabalpur, a journalist for the radio and *Nayā khũn* in Nagpur, unemployed in Allahabad and Calcutta, and finally managed to get a job as a lecturer at a degree college in Rajanandgaon in 1958 (after a belated MA in Hindi in 1953), a position which allowed him some relief from merciless poverty and frustration.

Throughout his adult life Muktibodh was financially responsible for his wife and children, brothers and ageing parents. His description of his ceaseless struggle for survival is bitterly laconic: 'I kept taking and giving up jobs. Teacher, journalist, teacher again, government service, non-government employment. Lower-middle class life, children, medical treatment, birth and death.' (Agyeya 1996a, p.19)

And yet, this struggle for daily bread never eroded Muktibodh's intellectual curiosity and engagement with ideas. He read with insatiable zest: Bergson, Gandhi and Marx; Jung and Adler; the romantic poems of Mahadevi Varma and Makhanlal, the novels of Balzac, Flaubert, Dostoyevski and Gorki. He pronounced himself a Marxist in *Tār saptak* in 1943 (Agyeya 1996a, p.22) and remained a firm believer in this ideology to his last breath. Muktibodh laid the foundations of the Progressive Writers' Association of Central India, and organised an anti-Fascist Conference in Indore in 1944. All his life he was connected with the struggles of the poor; Khare recounts how aggrieved Muktibodh was to read that surplus potatoes had been thrown into the ocean in America while so many people in India were starving. (Khare 1993, p.5)

His contemporaries describe him as emotional, good-hearted, straight-forward, innocent, generous, and obstinate. He worked with dedication, a sense of duty and perfectionism–sometimes he revised his poems twenty times and more before he was satisfied. Muktibodh was a mixture of rebel and traditionalist: he married for love against the wish of his parents and the expectations of society, and pronounced his commitment to the scientific, materialistic point of view (Agyeya 1996a, p.22), yet considered birth-control as a manifestation of capitalist evil (Bhatnagar 1976, p.20). He saw ugliness in beauty–he was the first poet in Hindi to characterise the face of the moon as 'crooked'; and beauty in ugliness–Shamsher tells of the compassion with which Muktibodh described to him a wayside thistle as soft, transparent and beautiful. (Jain 1964, p.19)

Muktibodh's poetry demands much from its readers; to borrow Ashok Vajpeyi's phrase, he is 'a difficult poet of a difficult time' (Vajpeyi 1994, p.1). His poems are typically very long and present a maze of dreams, fantasy and free associations. Muktibodh's canvases are vast: social life is intertwined with the individual's inner psyche. As Shamsher eloquently puts it: 'Muktibodh searches for the face of this era, buried under the rubble of history, and yet still alive' (Jain 1965, p.23). His palette is dark, sombre, or fiery: the rugged terrain, dark caves, forests and the deep wells of his mother's native town Ishagarh (Madhya Pradesh) are recurrent symbols in his poetry. His verses are packed with images of terror and chaos, suggesting a cruel, hollow, alienating capitalist civilisation, but also with symbols of his unshakeable belief in a golden future for the poor. Muktibodh frequently uses narratives and myths in order to give structure to his long poems. He writes in free verse, and his language is often prosaic. His poetry mixes dialectical materialism and romanticism, realism and fantasy, prosiness and lyricism. Summarising the undercurrents of Muktibodh's poetry, Shamsher asserts: 'Muktibodh crossed the romantic limitations of *Chāyāvād*, upheld Marxist philosophy, armed himself with the weapons of Experimentalism and advanced Nirala's pure humanism, as a free poet, above all parties and ideologies.' (ibid., p.26)

Apart from poetry Muktibodh wrote short stories, literary criticism, diaries and a novel. A second collection of his poems *Bhūrī-bhūrī khāk dhūl* (Grey dust and ashes) was published in 1980, followed by his complete works *Muktibodh racnāvalī* in six volumes. Though his *Kāmāyanī ek punarmūlyāṅkan* (Kamayani: a revaluation) and his *Ek lekhak kī dāyrī* (A writer's diary)[2] have established him as a very important voice in Hindi literary criticism, it is the spell of his poetry which has secured Muktibodh an honoured place in the Hindi literary pantheon.

The text of the poems is taken from Jain 1980 and Vajpeyi 1994. For a very informative introduction to Muktibodh's life, see Shamsher's preface to Jain 1965. Singh 1997 and Chaturvedi 1990 provide insightful discussions of Muktibodh's poetry, particularly of 'Ādhere mẽ'. For further translations of his poetry, see Misra 1967, pp.63–4, Mehrotra 1974, Dharwadker 1996, pp.29–30, Vajpeyi 1998, pp.39–47, Satchidanandan, 2000, pp.67–75 and *Indian horizons*, vol, 42, pp.32–9. A translation of 'Ādhere mẽ' has recently been published in *Hindi: Language, discourse, writing*, vol 2 (1), together with a few articles on the poem.

Notes and References

[1]   Muktibodh, 'Statement' in Agyeya 1996a, p.23.
[2]   Both of them are published in *Muktibodh racnāvalī*, Jain 1980, vol. 4.

Gajanan   Muktibodh

अंधेरे में

ज़िंदगी के. . .
　　कमरों में अँधेरे
　　　　लगाता है चक्कर
　　　　　　कोई एक लगातर ;
आवाज़ पैरों की देती है सुनाई
बार-बार . . . बार-बार,
वह नहीं दीखता . . . नहीं ही दीखता,
किंतु, वह रहा घूम
तिलिस्मी खोह में गिरफ़्तार कोई एक :
भीत-पार आती हुई पास से,
गहन रहस्यमय अंधकार-ध्वनि-सा
　　अस्तित्व जनाता
　　　　अनिवार कोई एक,
और, मेरे हृदय की धक-धक
पूछती है वह कौन
सुनाई जो देता, पर नहीं देता दिखाई !
इतने में अकस्मात् गिरते हैं भीत से
फूले हुए पलस्तर,
ख़िरती है चूनेभरी रेत
ख़िसकती है पपड़ियाँ इस तरह-
ख़ुद-ब-ख़ुद
कोई बड़ा चेहरा बन जाता है,
स्वयमपि
मुख बन जाता है दिवाल पर,
नुकीली नाक और
भव्य ललाट है,
दृढ़ हनु :
कोई अनजानी अन-पहचानी आकृति ।
कौन वह दिखाई जो देता, पर
नहीं जाना जाता है !!
कौन मनु ?
　. . .

वह रहस्यमय व्यक्ति
अब तक न पाई गई मेरी अभिव्यक्ति है,

पूर्ण अवस्था वह
निज-संभावनाओं , निहित प्रभाओं, प्रतिभाओं की
मेरे परिपूर्ण का आविर्भाव,
हृदय में रिस रहे ज्ञान का तनाव वह,
आत्मा की प्रतिमा ।

. . .

सूनि है राह , अजीब है फैलाव,
सर्द अँधेरा ।
ढीलि आँखों से देखते हैं विश्व
उदास तारे ।
हर बार सोच और हर बार अफ़सोस
हर बार फ़िक्र
के कारण बढ़े हुए दर्द का मानो कि दूर वहाँ, दूर वहाँ
अँधियारा पीपल देता है पहरा ।
हवाओं को निःसंग लहरों में काँपती
कुत्तों की दूर-दूर अलग-अलग आवाज़,
टकराती रहती सियारों की ध्वनि से ।
काँपती हैं दूरियाँ, गूँजते है फ़ासले
(बाहर कोई नहीं, कोई नहीं बाहर)
इतने मे अँधियारे सूने में कोई चीख़ गया है
रात का पक्षी
कहता है ː
'वह चला गया है,'
वह नहीं आएगा, आएगा ही नहीं
अब तेरे द्वार पर ।
वह निकल गया है गाँव में शहर में !
उसका तू ख़ोज अब
उसका तू शोध कर !
वह तेरी पूर्णतम परम अभिव्यक्ति,
उसका तू शिष्य है (यद्यपि पलातक . . .)
वह तेरी गुरु है
गुरु है . . .'

. . .

वह मेरे पास कभी बैठा ही नहीं था,
वह मेरे पास कभी आया ही नहीं था,
तिलिस्मी खोह में देखा था एक बार,
आख़िरी बार ही !
पर, वह जगत् की गलियों में घूमता है प्रतिपल
वह फटे-हाल रूप ।
विद्युलहरिल वही गतिमयता,
उद्विग्न ज्ञान-तनाव वह

सकर्मक प्रेम की वह अतिशयता
वही फटे-हाल रूप !!
परम अभिव्यक्ति
अविरत घूमती है जग में
पता नहीं जाने कहाँ, जाने कहाँ
वह है।
इसीलिए मैं हर गली में
और हर सड़क पर
झाँक-झाँक देखता हूँ हर एक चेहरा,
प्रत्येक गतिविधि,
प्रत्येक चरित्र,
व हर एक आत्मा का इतिहास,
हर एक देश व राजनीतिक स्थिति और परिवेश
प्रत्येक मानवीय स्वानुभूत आदर्श
विवेक-प्रक्रिया, क्रियागत परिणति !!
खोजता हूँ पठार . . . पहाड़. . . समुंदर
जहाँ मिल सके मुझे
मेरी वह खोई हुई
परम अभिव्यक्ति अनिवार
आत्म-संभवा।

In the dark[1]

In life's . . .
   dark chambers
      someone is pacing up and down
         ceaselessly;
I can hear the sound of his steps
again and again . . . again and again
I cannot see him . . . cannot see him
but he goes on wandering
Someone arrested in an enchanted cave;
Someone unstoppable
   asserts his existence
      like the echo of deep mysterious darkness,
resounding nearby, behind the wall.
And the beating of my heart
asks–Who is he
that I can hear, but cannot see?
Then bulging plaster
suddenly falls from the wall
Sand full of lime cracks
Flakes slip

a big face emerges
of its own accord
A silhouette appears on the wall–
Pointed nose,
magnificent brow,
firm chin;
An unknown unfamiliar shape.
Who is he
that I can see, but
cannot know!
Manu?[2]...
That mysterious man
is my expression which I haven't found yet
He is the ripeness
of my potential, latent brilliance, talents;
the realisation of my completeness
the tension of knowledge oozing in my heart
the image of my soul.

...

Empty road, strange expanse
cold darkness.
Sad stars observe the world
with indifferent eyes.
Pain grows
with every concern, every regret
every worry, as if guarded by
the dark pipal tree far far away.
Dogs' distant distinct barking
vibrates in the careless waves of the wind
constantly clashing with jackals' howling.
Distances tremble, interspaces echo
(Outside no one, no one outside)
Then somebody screams in the dark void–
A bird of the night
says:
'He's gone
he won't come back, won't come
to your door any more.
He's gone to villages and towns!
Search for him now,
examine him!
He's your absolute ultimate expression

you, his disciple (though fugitive. . .)
He's your teacher
teacher . . .'
. . .
He never sat next to me,
never even came to me,
once I saw him in an enchanted cave
it was the last time!
But he walks the lanes of this world ceaselessly
in tattered clothes
at the speed of lightning
He—anxious tension of knowledge,
abundance of vigorous love
in tattered clothes!
My ultimate expression
wanders in the world ceaselessly
I don't know where he is
Who does?
So I scrutinise every face
on every lane
and every street,
all actions,
all deeds,
the history of every soul,
every country, political situation and circumstance
every human self-perceived ideal,
the process of discrimination, the active transformation!
I search plateaus . . . mountains . . . oceans
wherever I might find
my lost
ultimate expression,
unstoppable,
self-born.

चांद का मुँह टेढ़ा है

नगर के बीचोबीच
आधी रात-अँधेरे की काली स्याह
शिलाओं से बनी हुई दिवालों के घेरों पर,
अहातों के काँच-टुकड़े-जमे-हुए
ऊँचे-ऊँचे कंधों पर, सिरों पर
चाँदनी की फैली हुई साँवलाई झालरें ।
कारख़ाना-अहाते के उस पार

कलमुँही चिमनियों के मीनार
उद्घार-चिह्नाकार।
मीनारों के बीचोबीच चाँद का है टेढ़ा मुँह
लटका,

मेरे दिल में खटका-
कहीं कोई चीख, कहीं बहुत बुरा हाल रे !!

अजीब है !!
गगन में करफ़्यू
धरति पर चुपचाप ज़हरीली छीः थूः,
पीपल के सुनसान घोसलों में पैठे हैं
कारतूस -छर्रे
जिससे के हवेली में
हवाओं के पल्लू भी सिहरे।
गंजे-सिर चाँद की सँवलाई किरनों के जासूस
साम-सूम नगर में धीरे-धीरे घूम-घाम
नगर के कोनों के तिकोनों में छुपे छुए
करते हैं महसूस
गलियों की हाय-हाय !!
चाँद की कनखियों की किरनों ने
नगर छान डाला है।
अँधेरे को आड़ -तिरछे काटकर
पीली-पीली पट्टियाँ बिछा दीं,
समय काला-काला है।

समीप विशालाकार अँधियाले ताल पर
सूनेपन की स्याही में डूबी हुई
चाँदनी भी सँवलाई हुई है।

शहर के बड़े-बड़े पुलों के
महराबों-नीचे बहुत नीचे उन
सिमटी हुई डरी हुई
बस्तियों के सुनमान उदास किनारों से लगकर
बहते-अटकते हुए
झरते-अटकते हुए
पथरीले नालों की काली-काली धार में
घराशायी चाँदनी के होंठ काले पड़ गए।

ह रिजन-बस्ती में, मंदिर के पास एक
कबीठ के धड़ पर,
मटमैले छप्परों पर,
बरगद की ऐंठी हुई अभरी हुई जड़ पर
कुहासे के भूतों के लटके
चूनर के चिथरे
अँगिया व घाघरे, फटी हुई चादरें

अटक गई जिनमें एक
व्यभिचारी टकटकी
गंजे सिर, टेढ़े-मुँह चाँद की ही कंजी आँख।

. . .

अजी, यह चाँदनी भी बड़ी मसख़री है
तिमंजिले की एक
खिड़की में बिल्लि के सफ़ेद धब्बे-सी
चमकती हुई वह
समेटकर हाथ-पाँव, किसी की ताक में
चुपचाप बैठी है।
धीरे-से उतरती है रास्तों पर
चढ़ती है छतों पर
गैलरी में घूम और खपरैलों पर चढ़कर
पेड़ों की शाख़ों की सहायता से आँगन में उतरकर
कमरों के हलके पाँव देखती है, खोजती है
जाने क्या ?
सड़कों के पेड़ों के गुंबदों पर चढ़कर
महल उलाँघकर, मुहल्ले पारकर
गलियों की गृहाओं में दबे-पाँव ख़ुफ़िया सुराग़ में
गुसचरी ताक में लगातार खोजती है
वह कौन
कंधों पर अँधेरे के चिपकाता कौन है
भड़कीले पोस्टर,
लंबे-चौड़े वर्ण और
बाँके-तिरछे घनघोर
लाल-नीले अक्षर !!

कोलतारी सड़क के बीचोबीच खड़ी हुई
गाँधी की मूर्ति पर बैठे हुए घुग्घू ने
एकाएक गला फाड़ गाना शुरू किया
हिचकी की ताल पर,
दुनिया की साँसों ने तब
मर जाना शुरू किया !!
टेलीफोन -खंभों थमे हुए तारों ने
सट्टे के ट्रंक-काल-सुर में
भर्राना और झनझनाना शुरू किया
काला स्याह कनटोप पहने हुए
आसमान बाबा ने
संकट पहचान
राम-राम-राम गुनगुनाना शुरू किया।
सचाई के अधजले मर्दों की सुनसान
चताओं की अधफूटी दहक में (अकस्मात्)

थरथरा उठते हैं पेड़ों पर प्रकाश के चिथड़े
बिंब-क्षेप करते हैं
अफसोसभरे गहरे दुखड़े
जिन्हें देख, जिन्हें सुन
किन्हीं अति-संस्कृत भूतों के गोल-गोल
मटकों-से चेहरों ने
नम्रता के घिघियाते स्वर में
दुनिया को हाथ जोड़
कहना शुरू किया-
'बुद्ध के स्तूप में
मानव के सपने
गड़ गए, गाड़े गए !!
ईसा के पंख सब
झड़ गए झाड़े गए
सत्य की देवदासी-अँगिया
उतारी गई
उधारी गई
सपनों की आँतें सब
चोरी गईं, फाड़ी गईं
बाकी सब खोल है
जिंदगी में झोल हैं

The moon's face is crooked[3]

In the middle of town
midnight—on the walls of pitch black rock,
on the high shoulders of enclosures, topped with broken glass, on
    the edges,
spread the inky fringes of moonlight
Across the factory enclosure
the minarets of black-faced chimneys—
Exclamation marks!
Between the minarets the moon's crooked face,
suspended,
in my heart, apprehension—
now a scream, now wretchedness!
It is strange!
Curfew in the sky
On the earth silent poisonous disgust
Desolate nests on the pipal tree
penetrated by pellets
so even the wind's borders shiver
in the mansions

Like spies the inky rays of the bald-headed moon
quietly wander about the black-skied city
Hidden in the triangles of the town's corners
they feel
the distress of the lanes!
The rays of the moon's side-glances
search the town
cut the darkness diagonally
and spread pale strips
Time is pitch black.
On the monstrous dark tank nearby
sunk in the blackness of the void
the moon too becomes dark.
Beneath the arches of town's great bridges,
deep down
touching the desolate sad banks
of the jammed, scared settlements,
the lips of the moon, resting on the ground, turn black
in the drifting-stopping
flowing-stopping
pitch-black current of the gravelly gutters.
In the settlement of the untouchables, near the temple,
hanging on the trunk of a wood-apple tree
on the dirty thatched roofs,
on the swollen coiled roots of the banyan tree
tatters of fog-ghosts' garments,
bodices, skirts, torn sheets
The light-coloured eye of the bald-headed, crooked-faced moon
staring viciously at them.

. . .

Look, this moonlight is also a great buffoon
shining
on a third-floor window
like a white spot on a cat
It's sitting silently
with paws folded, on the lookout for somebody.
Softly it drops to the roads
springs to the ceilings,
wanders the corridors, climbs the tiled roofs,
slips down the tree branches into tile courtyards
light-footed, surveying the rooms, searching for
who knows what?

Climbing up the cupolas of the trees on the streets
jumping over mansions, crossing neighbourhoods
stealthily in a secret search through the dens of lanes
it keeps seeking, spying, laying in wait.
Who is that?
Who is sticking onto the shoulders of darkness
showy posters?
Huge shapes
fearsome, slanting
red and blue letters!

The owl sitting on the statue of Gandhi
erect in the middle of a coal tar street
suddenly started singing at the top of its voice
at the beat of hiccups
World's breath
began to die away!
The wires held by telephone poles
began to croak and rattle
in the voice of transactions trunk calls.
Grandpa sky,
wearing a pitch black cap,
saw the crisis
and started muttering God's name.
In the flaring flames of the desolate pyres
of truth's half-burnt corpses (suddenly)
the tatters of light rose trembling above the trees,
casting shadows
like grievous tales of woe
seeing which, hearing which
the round, pot-like faces
of some cultured ghosts
started saying
in soft, whining voices
with hands folded in supplication to the world–
'The dreams of mankind
got buried, entombed
in the Buddhist stupas!
The wings of Jesus
were shed, torn away.
The bodice of the temple prostitute of truth
was removed, stripped off.
The bowels of all dreams, were cut, split open

The rest is hollow
life's cavity.'

बेचैन चील

बेचैन चील !!
उस-जैसा मैं पर्यटनशील
प्यासा-प्यासा,
देखता रहूँगा एक दमकती हुई झील
या पानी का कोरा झाँसा
जिसकी सफ़ेद चिल चिलाहटों में है अजीब
इनकार एक सूना !!

Restless kite

Restless kite!
Like it, I roaming,
dying of thirst,
will keep looking at the glittering lake
or the mere mirage of water
in whose white blazes
there is a strange, blank rejection.

Notes and References

1   'Ādhere mē' is Muktibodh's longest, most famous and arguably most obscure
poem. It stretches over 30 pages in the edition I have used. The selection presented
here includes the beginning and the end of the poem, and two extracts from parts
1 and 2. They all focus on the image of the 'ultimate expression', of man's lost
identity, the search for which is the central theme of this work.

'Ādhere mē' covers a large canvas of India's history before and after Independence.
If we try to unravel its intricate narrative thread it will guide us through the
appearance of a face on a wall and in a dark pond, of a man, bathed in blood-light
in a cave; the realisation that this man is the poetic protagonist's 'ultimate
expression' (part 1); the protagonist responding to the call of this man and searching
for him, guided by 'the bird of night' (part 2); a strange procession and a death
sentence given to the protagonist (part 3); martial law to put the people's revolution
down (part 4); the protagonist running for his life and looking at the 'diamonds' of
his 'anguish, experience, understanding' in a 'deep dark cave' (part 5); the
protagonist trying to escape again, seeing blood dripping from Tilak's statue and
encountering Gandhi, who hands him the infant of the future; the protagonist's
capture and torture; his release; his experience of the dangers of expression (part
6); the protagonist reading a pamphlet which shows him the way forward–the path
of communism (part 7); the protagonist waking up in the morning and seeing from
his balcony that the man–his 'ultimate expression'–is in the midst of the crowds',
'down there in the streets' (part 8).

This kind of 'decoding' of 'Ādhere mẽ' into a single narrative line does no justice to this complex poem, in which 'real' and allegorical are tightly knit. This intricate pattern intertwines: 'the "search and find motif" operating with enigmatic encounters. . . ; the classical dramaline of failure, guilt, oracle, task, catharsis and realisation. . . ; the time journey evolving from a "real" night setting through several. . . zones of darkness. . ., up to the eventual "real" light of the "morning"; the cleverly arranged geographical shifting between areas of outside and inside. . ., of urban and natural settings, corresponding with mental areas of "dream" and "wakefulness" and set against the protagonist's "real" movement from his dark, closed claustrophobic room to the sunlit veranda overlooking a busy street; the arrangement of historic and literary characters to enact the intellectual self-questioning in search of a guiding "guru", up to a point where the protagonist seems to represent nothing less than India ten years after independence.' (Lotz 2001, p.105). Once we start to follow this intricate pattern, to marvel at its colours and shapes, its complexity and richness, its images, we can understand why the prominent Hindi literary critic Namwar Singh has labelled this poem 'the grand finale of [Muktibodh's] poetic opus' and even 'the grand finale of the achievements of New Poetry'. (Singh 2001, p.118)

[2] Manu is a mythological figure who partly corresponds to the biblical and Koranic Adam. He is the progenitor of the world and its inhabitants, seen as son of or personification of Brahma, the Creator. Manu is the principal character of one of the most important works of the Chāyāvādī period, Prasad's epic Kāmāyanī, which Muktibodh has analysed in his Kāmāyanī: ek punarmūlyāṅkan (Kāmāyanī: a revaluation), see Jain 1980. pp.211-387.

[3] 'Cā̃d kā mūh terhā hai' is another long poem (15 pages in the edition I have used), divided into two parts. The two extracts I have included are both from the first part: the beginning of the poem and the end of the first part (without the last stanza); they are connected by the image of the moon. The extracts give a sense of the general tenor of this work, in which curfew rules over sky and earth (slight variations on 'Curfew in the sky/on the earth silent poisonous disgust' are repeated throughout the poem); the moon, with its 'crooked face' is a spy and no ordinary man is safe. The poem depicts compassionately the plight of the poor, who live under 'dirty thatched roofs' in 'jammed, scared settlements'. There is no hint of the usual romantic associations of the moon; instead the poet draws a powerful picture of contemporaneous reality as a realm of ugliness and terror.

Shamsher Bahadur Singh
1911–1993

Many literary critics have tried to label Shamsher, to find the 'right' epithet for his poetry: Marxist, progressive, imagist, experimentalist, surrealist, romantic, mystic, hermetic. For Ashok Vajpeyi, Shamsher is a 'a poets' poet' (Agrawal 1994, p.98)[1] for Sahi a 'poet of pure beauty' (ibid., p.99), for Muktibodh a 'poet of love'.(ibid., p.8), for Malayaja a 'poet of moods' (Chaturvedi 1990, p.87). Shamsher is all these things and more; his poetry and his personality encompass variety, multiplicity and contradiction. Shamsher is a Marxist and an experimentalist, a poet and an artist, a writer in Hindi and Urdu, a man of childlike innocence, peasant roots and refined sensibility.

Shamsher's ambiguous attitude towards progressivism has been the focus of much critical discourse. 'As soon as one decides to write about Shamsher one faces the problem if he should place him next to the [Marxist] Muktibodh or to the [experimentalist] Agyeya,' complains Vishvambhar 'Manav' ('Manav' 1978, p.245). After all, Shamsher has dedicated poems to both. Is Shamsher a Marxist? His statement in *Dūsrā saptak*, and the introductions to his collections and diaries testify to an aspiration to Marxist ideals, but simultaneously acknowledge his failure to reach them. The majority of his poems, among them his masterpieces, are not marked by Marxist ideology. As Sahi points out: 'Marxism remained limited to the margins of Shamsher's poetry' (Agrawal 1994, p.84).

It is not just the progressivist and the experimentalist fighting for dominance in Shamsher's works; another duality central to him is that of poet and artist. Muktibodh describes Shamsher's struggle to 'dismiss the artist enthroned in his heart and install the poet instead.' (ibid., part 2, p.57). But it is the painter who has crafted most of Shamsher's poems. He was interested in art from an early age, and attended the Ukil School of Art in Delhi; the painter's sensibility remains central to Shamsher throughout his life. He admits: 'I usually grasp things as a painting and try to transfer the first impression in words' (ibid., p.266), and 'the medium I have chosen alongside poetry, inside poetry, is that of abstract painting' (ibid., p. 291). It is this process of 'translating' visual art into poetry which makes some of Shamsher's lyrics elliptical, enigmatic, difficult to grasp: 'an impressionist artist gives place in his painting only to those parts which are extremely important. Completing his work only in a few brush-strokes he leaves the rest to the viewer's imagination' (Muktibodh in ibid., p.56). Silence is an eloquent part of painting and an important presence in Shamsher's poetry. Malayaja observes: 'Shamsher's art is the art of not saying' (ibid., p.36).

Shamsher's personality too encompasses opposites. His contemporaries describe him as innocent, honest, straightforward, loyal, warm, hospitable, generous, gentle, introvert, extremely shy, humble and unassertive; and yet also as possessing firmness, belief in his convictions, and an iron will to pursue his total dedication to poetry, despite the merciless financial difficulties he had to endure. Likewise, Shamsher's roots in the humble *jāt* community of cultivators contrast with his image as an urban and urbane middle-class man.

The name 'Shamsher Bahadur Singh' translates literally as 'sword brave lion', but Pradip Saksena compares the gentle, humble, shy man named so majestically with 'a butterfly' (ibid., p.39). Shamsher himself mocks this incongruity between his personality and his name, picturing himself as being of *nām bare darśan thore* (grand name, modest appearance). His 'butterfly'-like shyness and humility lay behind his desperate effort to avoid the spotlight of public attention and the extremely belated publication of his works. His first collection, modestly titled *Kuch kavitāē* (Some poems), appeared as late as 1959, and even then thanks only to the tireless insistence of his friends and admirers. It is not surprising that a man so free of affectation should conjure up the image of an innocent child. Jaya Shrivastav pictures him 'riding a red children's tricycle among his solemnly striding fellow-writers and artists' (ibid., p.224). Shamsher himself muses in his diaries: 'The artist is nothing but a child. This is his comedy and his tragedy' (*Kalpanā*, January 58, p.52), and proceeds to translate *Alice in wonderland*.

Another quality Shamsher shares with children is an insatiable curiosity and desire to learn. He was fluent in Urdu, Hindi, Persian and English, and studied Spanish, French, German and Sanskrit. He did not have the opportunity to travel–his only trip abroad was to the USSR in 1978–but through his reading he 'visited' many faraway places. This thirst for knowledge is reflected in his advice to those who aspire to be poets: be aware of the social and political situation in your country, learn science, study different languages and literatures and be acquainted with the world's literary heritage ('Hone vāle mahākavi ke lie', in Agrawal 1994, part 2, pp.31–5).

The desire to educate himself was one element in Shamsher's single-minded dedication to poetry. He believed in the importance of the poet's freedom, and tried to compromise as little as possible, notwithstanding his poverty. Moving from one place to the next–Allahabad, Bombay, Delhi–he made a meagre living as an editor of different journals: *Rūpabh, Māyā, Nayā Sāhitya, Nayā path*,

Kahānī, Manohar kahāniyā, and of an Urdu-Hindi dictionary. The rest of his time he wrote: poems, essays, diaries, stories and translations from Urdu and English.

Eleven collections of Shamsher's poems have been published (including his contribution to Agyeya's *Dūsra saptak*). He used many different poetic forms—songs, lyrics, sonnets, *rubāīs, gazals,* free verse—in Hindi and Urdu. Shamsher saw himself as standing 'between the rivers of Hindi and Urdu' (*maī urdū aur hindī kā doāb hū,* 'Bārh 1948' in Singh 1994, p.80) and brought into Hindi the idiom, sensuousness and melody of his native Urdu. The topics of his poems are varied: the 'recognition of life sleeping in ordinary events' (Chaturvedi 1990, p.87), society, politics; he dedicated more than eighty poems to his contemporaries, and wrote about Van Gogh, Picasso, Bach and Chinese pictograms. However, nature and love are Shamsher's topoi and the themes of his most successful lyrics. Despite his life-long solitude (his mother died when he was nine, his wife shortly after their marriage), he painted the most 'varied and gentle pictures of love in *Nayī Kavitā*' (Muktibodh in Agarwal 1994, p.8). But the word which encapsulates the essence of his poetry is 'beauty'. In *Dūsrā saptak* Shamsher asserts: 'the embodiment of beauty is in front of us at every moment' (Agyeya 1996b, p.87). Shamsher's poetry is a vivid reminder of beauty's omnipresence.

Poems taken from Singh 1988 and Namwar Singh 1994. Agrawal 1994 is a very informative volume of interviews with and about Shamsher, recollections of his contemporaries, Shamsher's previously unpublished work and literary criticism. *Hindi: Language, discourse, writing,* vol. 1 (3-4) is partly dedicated to Shamsher. Shamsher's poetry has been translated in Mishra 1967, pp.37, 61, 99 and 107; Dharwadker 1996, pp.145-6; Vajpeyi 1998, pp.9–17; Satchidanandan 2000, pp.39–43 and *Indian horizons,* vol. 42, pp.40–3.

Notes and References

[1] These are actually Shamsher's words. In his diary of 11.03.1963 he writes, 'Some writers are writers' writers... Among the poets: Pant, Nirala ... Agyeya, Shamsher! (Poets' poets)', *Kalpanā,* December 1964, p.63.

Shamsher Bahadur Singh

एक पीली शाम

एक पीली शाम
    पतझर का ज़रा अटका हुआ पत्ता
शांत
मेरी भावनाओं में तुम्हारे मुखकमल
कृश म्लान हारा-सा
    (कि मैं हूँ वह
मौन दर्पण में तुम्हारी कहीं ?)
      वासना डूबी
      शिथिल पल में
      स्नेह काजल में
      लिए अद्भुत रूप-कोमलता
अब गिरा अब गिरा वह अटका हुआ आँसू
सांध्य तारक-सा
    अतल में ।

A pale evening

A pale evening
    an autumn leaf lingering
serene
In my thoughts your lotus face
fine, dejected, lost
    (Am I the one
in your still mirror somewhere?)
    Desire sank
    in the languid moment
    in the kohl of affection
    carrying beauty's wondrous softness
That lingering tear about to fall
like a twilight star
    in the unfathomable.

उषा

प्रात नभ था बहुत नीला शंख जैसे
भोर का नभ

राख से लीपा हुआ चौका
(अभी गीला पड़ा है)
बहुत काली सिल ज़रा से लाल केसर से
कि जैसे धुल गई हो
स्लेट पर या लाल खड़िया चाक
मल दी हो किसी ने
नील जल में या किसी की
            गौर झिल मिल देह
जैसे हिल रही हो।
और . . .
     जादू टूटता है इस उषा का अब
     सूर्योदय हो रहा है।

Dawn

Early morning sky–like a deep blue conch shell

sky at daybreak

Kitchen floor cleaned with ashes

[still wet]

a pitch black stone

as if washed with red saffron

or a streak of red chalk

crushed on a slate

or a fair glistening body

swaying in the blue waters

and . . .

    The spell of this dawn breaks

    Sunrise is coming.

पूर्णिमा का चाँद

चाँद निकला बादलों से पूर्णिमा का।
     गल रहा है आसमान।
एक दरिया उमड़कर पीले गुलाबों का
     चूमता है बादलों के झिलमिलाते
     स्वप्न जैसे पाँव।

Full moon

The moon emerged from the clouds, full

    The sky dissolving

A river of yellow roses swells

and kisses the shimmering dreamlike feet
of the clouds.

सुबह
जो कि सिकुड़ा हुआ बैठा था, वो पत्थर
सजग-सा होकर पसरने लगा
आप से आप।

Morning

That stone, sitting shrivelled,
woke up and stretched
of its own accord.

धूप कोठरी के आइने में खड़ी
धूप कोठरी के आइने में खड़ी
हँस रही है

पारदर्शी धुप के पर्दे
मुस्कराते
मौन आँगन में

मोम-सा पीला
बहुत कोमल नभ
एक मधुमक्खी हिलाकर फूल को
बहुत नन्हा फूल
उड़ गई

आज बचपन का
उदास मा का मुख
याद आता है।

Sunlight standing in the mirror of the hut

Sunlight standing in the mirror of the hut
laughing

Blinds of translucent light
smiling
in the silent courtyard

Soft sky
the colour of wax

A honey-bee swaying a flower
a tiny flower
flew away

Childhood memory of
mother's sad face
now

प्रेयसी
एक
तुम मेरी पहलि प्रेमिका हो
जो आइने की तरह साफ़
बदन के माध्यम से ही बात करती हो
और शायद (शायद)
मेरी बात   साफ़-साफ़
समझती भी हो।
प्यारी,   तुम कितनी प्यारी हो।
        वह काँसे का चिकना बदन हवा में हिल रहा है
        हवा हौले-हौले नाच रही है,
            इसलिए....
- तुम भी मेरी आँखों में
(स्थिर रूप में साकार रहते हुए भी)
हौले -हौले अनजाने रूप में
नाच रही हो
        हौले-हौले
हौले-हौले यह कायनात हिल रही है

दो
गंदुमी गुलाब की पाँखुड़ियाँ
खुली हुई हैं
आँखों की शबनम
        दूर चारों तरफ़
            हँस रही है
यह मीठी हँसी
        जो मेरे अंदर घुलती जा रही है
तुम हो।
तुम्हारा सुडौल बदन एक आबशार है
जिसे मैं एक ही जगह खड़ा देखता हूँ
ऐसा चिकना और गतिमान
ऐसा   मूर्त   सुंदर   उज्जवल

तीन
यह पूरा
        कोमल काँसे में ढला
            गोलाईयों का आईना
मेरे सीने से कसकर भी
        आज़ाद है

जैसे किसी खुले बाग़ में
    सुबह की सादा
            भीनी-भीनी हवा
यह तुम्हारा ठोस बदन
        अजब तौर से
            मेरे अंदर बस गया है।

Beloved

1.

You are my first lover
who speaks with her body alone
clearly like a mirror
and perhaps (perhaps)
also understands
my words   clearly.
Beloved, you are so precious,
        That smooth bronze body of yours is swinging in the wind,
        the wind is dancing slowly
                and so . . .
−You too are dancing
in my eyes
slowly
(even in the stillness of your body)
        slowly in a strange way
slowly the universe is swinging.

2.

Rose-petals of wheat-colour
opened
eye-dew
all around
smiling
This sweet smile
which melts inside me
is you.
Your graceful body is a fountain
which I see motionless
so sleek and agile,
so tangible splendid radiant

3.

This whole
    mirror of curves

      cast in supple bronze
   is free even in my embrace
like pure
      light morning breeze
         in an unlocked garden.
This sculpted body of yours
   dwells in me
   wondrously.

तुमने मुझे

तुमने मुझे और गूँगा बना दिया
एक ही सुनहरि आभा-सी
      सब चीज़ों पर छा गई

मैं और भी अकेला हो गया

तुम्हारे साथ गहरे उतरने के बाद
      मैं एक ग़ार से निकला
            अकेला, खोया हुआ और गूँगा
अपनी भाषा तो भूल ही गया जैसे
चारों तरफ़ की भाषा ऐसी हो गई
      जैसे पेड़ों पौधों की होती है
      नदियों में लहरों की होती है
हज़रत आदम के यौवन का बचपना
हज़रत हौव्वा की युवा मासूमियत
कैसी भी ! कैसी भी !
ऐसा लगता है जैसे
तुम चारों तरफ़ से मुझसे लिपटी हुई हो
मैं तुम्हारे व्यक्तित्व के मुख में
आनंद का स्थायी ग्रास . . . हूँ
मूक ।

You have made me

You have made me more mute
like a golden gleam
   diffused in everything
I've become more lonely
I descended with you into the depths
   and emerged from a cavern
      alone, lost, mute.
My language I forgot
and spoke the tongue of everything around me
   of trees and plants

of river ripples
The childishness of Mr Adam's youth
The young innocence of Miss Eve
Anyhow!
It seems
that you are enfolding me from all directions
I, the lasting morsel of bliss
in the mouth of your uniqueness . . . am
speechless.

कवि घंघोल देता है

कवि घंघोल देता है
    व्यक्तियों के जल
हिला-मिला देता
    कई दर्पणों के जल
जिसका दर्शन हमें
    शान्त कर देता है
और गंभीर
अंत में

A poet stirs

A poet stirs
    the streams of men
Mixes
    the lakes of many mirrors–
A sight which
    makes us serene
and profound
in the end.

I will have the whole of life
don't give me this 'at least'-talk.[1]

Raghuvir Sahay
1929–1990

These two lines capture the quintessence of Raghuvir Sahay's spirit: his commitment to life in its entirety. His appetite for 'the whole of life' urged him to choose journalism as his professional field: as a special correspondent for All India Radio and for the *Navbhārat Times,* and as chief editor of the Hindi newsweekly *Dinmān,* he was at the centre of the events of the day for four decades. Raghuvir Sahay never saw any disparity between his commitment to reality and his loyalty to literature. On the contrary, as he asserts in *Nayī Kavitā* 4: 'the first condition for being an artist is to fully participate in all areas of life' (Sahay 1959, p.34). 'Poetry should be rooted in reality', he adds in his statement in *Dūsrā saptak* (Agyeya 1996b, p.139). He remained true to his determination to 'be fully alert to the social reality (ibid., p.138) in all his writing: in his political journalism and literary criticism (he worked also as an editor of the literary journals *Pratīk* and *Kalpanā*) as well as in his short stories, philosophical essays and poetry.

Raghuvir Sahay's deep-rootedness in 'reality' started very early. Born in 1929, he grew up in the highly charged atmosphere of the struggle for Independence. It is hardly surprising then that the writers who inspired him most in his childhood were social realists like Premchand and Dickens (Senkevich 1983, p.5). Yet his commitment to society was never tainted by dogmatism: he never joined a political party. In *Dūsrā saptak* Raghuvir Sahay recounts Shamsher's assertion that 'three things are truly important in life: oxygen, Marxism and those features of ours which reflect the ordinary people' (Agyeya 1996b, p.138). However, Sahay immediately warns of the dangers of allowing ideology to rule creativity: 'But Marxism shouldn't be put on top of poetry like a cover.' (ibid.)

The symbiosis of reality and writing is reflected both in the subject matter and language of Raghuvir Sahay's poetry. He writes of ordinary things, of experiences which we can all recognise as our own, of familiar images and episodes: 'I have always tried to feel the unique fragrance of experiences which on the surface seem very ordinary, and to help society sense this fragrance too' (Ray 1997, p.244). In his most successful poems, like 'Today anew', included here, he does just that: uncovers the magic of the ordinary, of the everyday.

And yet his sensitivity to the 'fragrance' of the commonplace is not sealed off from the stench of its ugliness. His poems are typically short, but they reflect life in all its diversity: love, nature, families, illness, death, murder, poverty, hypocrisy, corruption, etc. etc. His verses are records of the hardship the ordinary man endures in contemporary society, and yet a desire to live and a faith in life are undercurrents in his poetry. As Ramsvarup Chaturvedi points out, in a playful paraphrase of the titles of Sahay's two first collections of poems Sīrhlyō par dhūp mē̃ (On the sunlit stairs) and Ātmahatyā ke viruddha (Against suicide): 'It is only natural for a man who sits on sunlit stairs to be against suicide' (Chaturvedi 1990, p.35). Though 'an anxious young man'[2] who believes that 'writing is the worst wound one can afflict on oneself. . . a huge pain and a huge sacrifice' (Sahay 1997, p.151), Raghuvir Sahay clearly states that 'to accept boredom, resentment, suffocation, helplessness and weariness is defeat for the artist' since these are 'facts of our age, not the truth of our age' (Sahay 1959, p.34).

Compassion and irony are the two poles of the emotional spectrum of Raghuvir Sahay's poetry. On the one hand he feels deeply for the ordinary person: oppressed women, bank clerks, rickshaw-pullers, coolies, the common voter. On the other hand he is deeply critical of the crowd which strangles individuality, of the hollowness of society and politics, of the maladies of corruption, deceit and hypocrisy. A recurring motif in Sahay's poetry, especially in his third collection Hamso, hamso jaldīhamso (Laugh, laugh, laugh quickly), is that of sham laughter as social mimicry. The force of irony intensifies with Raghuvir Sahay's development as a poet: whereas his first collection is influenced by the lyrical miniature devoted to love and nature, by tanka and haiku, many of his late poems are social satires charged with pain.

Sahay's commitment to reality and to the struggles of ordinary people affect not only the subject matter of his poetry but also its language. The most striking quality of Sahay's language is its ability to communicate. He uses a simple, straightforward everyday vocabulary, a vocabulary accessible to the ordinary man about whom he writes. As Agyeya points out in his introduction to Sīrhiyō par dhūp mē̃: 'In [Sahay's] poetry there is not even a single line which fails to communicate, which is obscure or difficult to understand'. However, it is easy to be deceived by the simplicity of Raghuvir Sahay's language; it imitates the rhythm and patterns of everyday speech, but it is skilfully chiselled. Even his use of conjuncts and particles, such as balki (but rather), aur (and, but), hī (precisely, merely), suggest an idiomatic mastery. The sheer output of this poet is staggering: more than ten books of poetry, essays, short stories, innumerable journalistic pieces and translations of fiction, poetry and drama from Poland, Hungary, Yugoslavia and England. One of his critics calls him *a yugāntarkārī kavi*, an epoch-making poet (Sharma 1994, p.5), and this is not a misplaced compliment. Raghuvir Sahay's poetry is a milestone in the development of *Nayī Kavitā*. As Ramsvarup Chaturvedi points out, 'If the ability to charge ordinary events and ordinary language with new power has become *Nayī Kavitā*'s special mark, much credit for that is due to Raghuvir Sahay.' (Chaturvedi 1990, p.38)

The text of the poems is taken from Sahay 1985, 1989a, 1989b, 1997 and Sharma 1994. An interview with Raghuvir Sahay is published in Ray 1997; Chaturvedi 1990 is a sensitive analysis of Sahay's poetic diction. Translations in Misra 1967, pp.32; Weissbort 1994, pp.1–9; Dharwadker 1996, pp.105–6; Vajpeyi 1998, pp.79–87; Ramakrishnan 1999, pp.167–9; Satchidanandan 2000, pp.167–70; *Indian horizons*, vol. 42, pp.49–50 and *Indian literature* 153, pp.11–18.

Notes and References

1   हम तो सारा का सारा लेंगे जीवन
    'कम से कम वालि बात न हम से कहिए'
    (from *Hamne yah dekhā*, Sahay 1997, p.78).

2   In his unpaginated introduction to *Sirhi yō par dhūp mē* Agyeya remarks: '[when introduced to Raghuvir Sahay] I mentally classified him as an anxious young man. Today too I think that he is exactly that, and I firmly believe that the anxious young man is much more mature and constructive than his successor, the angry young man.'

Raghuvir Sahay

आज फिर
आज फिर शुरू हुआ जीवन।
आज मैंने एक छोटी सी सरल-सी कविता पढ़ी।
आज मैंने सूरज को डूबते देर तक देखा।
आज मैंने शीतल जल से जी भर स्नान किया।
आज एक छोटी-सी बच्ची आयी , किलक मेरे कन्धे चढ़ी
आज मैंने आदि से अन्त तक एक पूरा गान किया।
आज जीवन फिर शुरू हुआ।

Today anew

Today life started anew.
Today I read a short, simple poem.
Today I watched the sun set for a long time.
Today I bathed to my heart's content in cool water.
Today a little girl came and shouting with delight climbed onto
    my shoulders.
Today I sang a whole song, from beginning to end.
Life started anew today.

पानि के संस्मरण
कौंध। दूर घोर वन में मूसलाधार वृष्टि
दुपहर : घना ताल : ऊपर झुकी आम की डाल
बयार : खिड़की पर खड़े, आ गयी फुहार
रातः उजली रेती के पार; सहसा दिखी शान्त नदी गहरी
मन में पानि के अनेक संस्मरण है।

Memories of water

Flash. Torrents of rain in a dense distant forest
Noon: Brimful pond: Above it a mango branch bowing
Wind: Standing at the window, drizzle starts
Night: Across the shimmering sand; a calm, deep river suddenly
    visible
In my mind there are many memories of water.

वसन्त

वही आदर्श मौसम
और मन में कुछ टूटता-सा :
अनुभव से जानता हूँ कि यह वसन्त है।

Spring

That classic season
Something breaking in my heart:
I know from experience–this is spring.

मैदान में

अँधेरा यहाँ
अँधेरा नहीं है
एक ख़ास तरह का चाँदना है
और न तू गोरी है

तू
एक लुनाई है डबडबायी हुई
काले
सिर्फ़ तेरे केश हैं
सूने मैदान में हम नही हैं
सिर्फ़ एक दिशा है
और गति है
और जिसमें ठिठके खड़े थे हम वह क्षण था
इसके बाद रोशनियाँ शहर की दिखायी देंगी।

In the field

Darkness here
is not darkness
but unusual moonlight
Nor are you fair

You are
beauty, brimming
Black
Only your hair

In this desolate field there is no 'us',
only space
and movement
and the moment in which we stood still
Then the city lights will come into sight.

सेब बेचना

मैंने कहा डपटकर
ये सेब दागी है
नहीं नहीं साहब जी
उसने कहा होता
आप निश्चिन्त रहें
तभी उसे खाँसी का दौरा पड़ गया
उसका सीना थामे खाँसी यही कहने लगी

Selling apples

I told him off,
'These apples have specks!'
'No, no, Sir',
He would have said,
'Don't you worry!'
But a fit of coughing overtook him,
seizing his chest the cough started saying it.

अकेली औरत

मोहन भीमार पड़ा
कमला को लगा कि वह अब सारी दुनिया को
छोड़कर उसके पास आया है

दो दिन ऐसा रहा
फिर मोहन रोग के एकांत के भीतर
और कहीं चला गया
कमला फिर अकेलि रह गयी कमला

Woman alone

Mohan fell ill
It seemed to Kamla that he had left the whole world
and come to her

This continued for two days
Then Mohan went somewhere else
inside the seclusion of his illness
Kamla was alone again, Kamla.

मनुष्य-मछलि युद्ध

जो मछलियाँ मीठे पानी में रह रही हैं
उन्हें हम समुद्र में डाल रहे हैं
क्योंकि मीठे पानी की मछलियाँ बिकती हैं

क्योंकि हम समुद्र से मछलियाँ पकड़तें हैं
क्योंकि हमारी नावें विकराल हैं
नदी में समाती नहीं

हम मछलियाँ पकड़ते हैं क्योंकि उन्हें
डब्बे में बन्द कर बेचेंगे
डब्बे में बन्द मछली हमारे लोकतंत्र का प्रतिक है
हर एक के लिए ताज़ा मछली की जगह उपलब्ध
हम विज्ञान को जीत रहे हैं
मछलि को डब्बे में बन्द करने के लिए
उस मछलि को मीठे पानी में न रहने देने के लिए विधि आविष्कार कर रहे हैं

मगर विज्ञान हमको जो आँकड़ देता है
वे बताते हैं कि मछलियों में समुद्र से
लौटकर मीठे पानी में जाने की अदम्य इच्छा है
हम मछली की नस्ल तगड़ी कर रहे हैं

ताकि वह स्वादू हो और महँगी भी
मछली तगड़ी हो रही है और मीठे पानी में
लौट आने को ताकत से तड़प रही है

हम विज्ञान से इन नतीजों पर पहुँचे हैं
कि हमें मछली को समुद्र में डालकर
उसे इतनी जल्दी मार लेना होगा
कि वह नदी में फिर न आने पाए।

War between men and fish

Fish which inhabit fresh water
we are taking to the sea
Because fresh-water fish sells
Because we catch fish in the sea
Because our boats are monstrous,
too large for rivers.

We catch fish to sell it
sealed in tins
Fish sealed in tins is a symbol of our democracy,
available to everyone instead of fresh fish.

We are conquering science
in order to seal fish in tins
We are inventing ways not to let fish live in fresh water.

But science produces statistics
which state that fish have an irrepressible urge
to go back from sea to fresh water.

We are making the fish stocks more sturdy
so that it's tasty and costly
Fish are becoming sturdy and writhing energetically
to go back to fresh water.

Thanks to science we have reached the conclusion
that we should kill the fish immediately
after taking them to the sea
so that they can't return to the river.

व्यावहारिक लोग

एक दिन घर लौटा
हाथ में किताब थी
और फूलगोभी थी
वाह, कविता मिली

आजकल किताब फूलगोभी-सी नरम है

और फूलगोभी है आजकल की किताब-सी नीरस
तुरंत एक सुंदरी से कहा जा करके
देखिए अदलबदल लीजिए आप इन दोनों को
वह नहीं समझी

लोग बहुत व्यावहारिक हो गये हैं
कोई ऊलजलूल नहीं बोलते
एक मुनाफ़ाख़ोर सभ्यता में मज़ाक की जगह नहीं रह गयी
(मनोरंजन की है जो नफ़रत से पैदा हो)
कोई चीज़ अपनी जगह से मत सरकाओ
व्यापारी व्यवस्था को उसकी ज़रूरत है
फूलगोभी पढ़ने और किताब ख़ाने से लाभ क्या होगा ?

Practical people

One day I returned home
In my hands a book
and a cauliflower
Wow! What a poem!

Nowadays books are as tender as cauliflower
and cauliflower as bland as books.
Immediately I advised a beauty,
'Look, you should swap the two over'
She didn't get it.

People have become very practical
They don't speak rubbish
A profiteers' society has no room for jokes

(only for entertainment, born of spite)
It's important for the business order
to keep everything in its place
What would one gain reading cauliflower or eating books?

फूट

हिंदू और सिख में
बंगाली असमिया में
पिछड़े और अगड़े में :
पर इनसे बडी फूट
जो मारा जा रहा और जो बचा हुआ
उन दोनों में है ।

Rift

Between a Hindu and a Sikh
A Bengali and an Assamese
A backward and a forward:
Rift deeper than these—
between a victim
and a survivor.

*The main attraction of Saxena's poetry, at least for me, lies in his passionate
drive to expand and deepen his sight. . . Sarveshwar's insistence to investigate
what is behind the visible. This drive is the rebellion of a capable man against
empty forms. That which is visible, which is on the surface is not false or unreal,
yet the insistence of the poet is to free the essence behind the membrane of the
forms. In the root of his drive is profound faith in life. This is the second
characteristic of Saxena's poetry. This faith allows Saxena to see life in its
completeness—completeness which encompasses incompleteness, error,
meaninglessness and division.*

(Agyeya 1955, p.34)

Sarveshwar Dayal Saxena
1927–1983

Agyeya's assertion that Saxena's poetry reflects life in its entirety is in harmony
with Saxena's own belief that 'any topic in the world should be accepted as a
possible topic of poetry' (Agyeya 1996c, p.213). This is a belief that he sets out
to realise in his work. He writes very private lyrics: about the pain and joy of
love, man's communion with nature, the tie with the village of his childhood,
the agony of loneliness; but he also writes 'public' verse–satires baring the
meaninglessness and horror of war, hypocrisy and political corruption, poems
drawing a 'uniform torture-stricken picture of Man' (Lutze 1985, p.57) in a
cold, dehumanised civilisation. His poetry is often political, sometimes
slogan-like, and yet never dogmatic. 'I am not a member of any political party'–
says Saxena–'because no political party is with the common man, however
much it may use his name'. (ibid., p.56)

Saxena's life was that of a common man. He was born in Basti (UP), a place
which he described vividly in many of his poems. His parents were teachers
and the family fought an endless battle with poverty. He was educated in Basti,
Benares and Allahabad, where he completed an MA in 1949. His short career
as a schoolteacher was followed by five years as a clerk. After that he became a
professional journalist; like Raghuvir Sahay, he worked in All India Radio, and
then as an editor of the Hindi newsweekly *Dinmān*. After nearly two decades
there he became the editor of *Parāg*, a Hindi magazine for children.

Saxena's last job, together with his own writing of poetry and plays for
children, and his fathering of two daughters speak of his connection with

children. As with Shamsher Bahadur Singh, Saxena too is portrayed as having a child-like nature–his fellow-poet and friend, Kunwar Narain describes Saxena's honesty and artlessness, but also his child-like surrender to sulking or joy (Narain 1998, p.209). A manifestation of this emotional impulsiveness was Saxena's total intolerance of any criticism of his work, as demonstrated by his angry defence of his poetry against Agyeya's comments that he lacked technical skill, due to deficient discipline of expression, and that his verses, with their ordinary colloquial language and the rhythm of prose, were devoid of beauty (Agyeya 1996c, p.214).

Agyeya's criticism highlights the characteristics of Saxena's poetry which are at the root of both his success and his failure. As Saxena himself says: 'I write a poem whenever the heat of feeling reaches boiling point' (Lutze 1985, p.58). The result is that his poetry is ruled by emotions, and is sometimes unabashedly sentimental. Saxena's idiom is colloquial Hindi, with no partiality for Sanskrit borrowings. His aim is to 'write simple verse for the illiterates of [his] country'; and in his effort to do this he employs colloquial speech and 'images and symbols from the common man's everyday life' (ibid., p.57). This modern idiom which makes poetry out of the language of ordinary conversations is one of Saxena's achievements, but when its rhythm is also that of prose, the poetry seems to disappear. Similarly, the use of common symbols undermines the poetic qualities of his verses: *kaccī sarak* (unsealed road) and its alternative *pakkā rājmārg* (asphalt highway), for example, are perhaps too obvious to be really successful symbols of Indian village culture and foreign civilisation, respectively.

Saxena was a versatile and prolific writer. In his relatively short life he published many pieces of journalism and about twenty books: nine collections of poetry (apart from his contribution to Agyeya's *Tīsrā saptak*), short stories, novels, poetry and plays for children, and a travelogue. He was honoured with several awards, among them the acclaimed Sahitya Akademi Award.

'If through my poetry I can communicate the suffering of the common man of my country, of my world, I shall be satisfied, for this will mean to me no less than that in this century I have proved my existence.' (ibid., p.58). At the beginning of a new century, we can confidently say that Saxena's work, in particular his poetry, is powerful testimony of his 'existence'.

The text of the poems is taken from Saxena 1966, Saxena 1994 and Shukla 1996. Munshi 1989 is a book of translations of Saxena's poetry. For further translations see Mishra 1967, pp.48–9 and 108–9; Lutze 1985, pp.52–5; Dharwadker 1996, pp.131–2; Vajpeyi 1998, pp.73-8, Ramakrishnan, 1999, pp.198–203, and Satchidanandan 2000, pp.155–9. Chaturvedi 1990 (pp.17–29) and Ray 1997 (pp.182–92) are discussions of Saxena's poetry.

Sarveshwar Dayal Saxena

पाँच नगर प्रतिक

दिल्ली :
कच्चे रंगों में नफ़ीस
चित्रकारी की हुई, कागज़ की एक डिबिया
जिस में नकली हीरे की अँगूठी
असली दामों के कैशमेमो में लिपटी हुई रखी है ।

लखनऊ :
शृंगारदान में पड़ी
एक पुरानी खाली इत्र की शीशी
जिस में अब महज़ उस की कार्क पड़ी सड़ रही है ।

बनारस :
बहुत पुराने तागों में बँधी एक तावीज़,
जो एक तरफ़ से खोल कर
भाँग रखने की डिबिया बना ली गयी है ।

इलाहाबाद :
एक छूछी गंगाजली
जो दिन-भर दोस्तों के नाम पर
और रात में कला के नाम पर
उठायी जाती है ।

बसती :
गाँव के मेले में किसी
पनवाड़ी के दुकान का शीशा
जिस पर इतनी धूल जम गयी है
कि अब कोई भी अक्स दिखायी नहीं देता ।

Five town-symbols

Delhi[1]:
A paper casket, exquisitely decorated
with colours that run.
In it a fake diamond ring
wrapped in a cash memo for the price of a real one.

Lucknow:
Lying in a make-up case
an old, empty perfume flask
In it nothing but its cork, rotting away.

Benares:
An amulet, tied to an ancient thread,
which opens on one side
and turns into a capsule for drugs.

Allahabad:
An empty pitcher for Ganges water
which is raised
all day long in the name of friends
and at night in the name of art.

Basti:
The mirror of a betel-seller's shop
at a village fair
on which so much dust has settled
that no reflection can be seen.

रात में वर्षा

मेरी साँसों पर मेघ उतरने लगे हैं,
आकाश पलकों पर झुक आया है,
क्षितिज मेरी भुजाओं से टकराता है,
आज रात वर्षा होगी ।
कहाँ हो तुम ?

मैंने शीशे का एक बहुत बड़ा एकवेरियम
बादलों के ऊपर आकाश में बनाया है,
जिस में रंग-बिरंगी असंख्य मछलियाँ डाल दी हैं,
सारा सागर भर दिया है ।
आज रात वह एकेरियम टूटेगा –
बौछारों की एक-एक बूँद के साथ
रंगीन मछलियाँ गिरेंगी ।
कहाँ हो तुम?

मैं तुम्हें बूँदों पर उड़ती
धारों पर चढ़ती-उतरती
झकोरों में दौड़ती, हाँफती,
उन असंख्य रंगीन मछलियों को दिखाना चाहता हूँ
जिन्हें मैंनं अपने रोम-रोम की पुलक से आकार दिया है ।

Rain at night[2]

Clouds start descending on my breath,
the sky lowers on my eyelids,
the horizon collides with my arms—
it will rain tonight.

Where are you?
I have made a huge glass aquarium
in the sky, above the clouds
and put there countless colourful fish,
filled the entire ocean.
Tonight this aquarium will break–
And with every drop of heavy shower
colourful fish will rain.
Where are you?

I want to show you these fish,
soaring on the drops,
going up and down the streams,
rushing in the torrents, gasping–
the countless, colourful fish
which I've shaped from my body's rapture.

अकेलापन

सूनी राह में दीखी
एक अकेली टहनी
मैंने उसे दो टुकड़े कर
पास-पास रख दिया।

Loneliness

A lonely twig
lying on an empty road
I split it in two
and placed the pieces side by side.

दरवाज़े बंद हैं

दरवाजे बंद हैं
घर में कोई नहीं हैं
सिवा स्मृतियों के।
दरारों से आई रोशनी

ख़ामोशी की पसलियों-सी
अभरी है
दीवारों पर।

नथुनों से दिमाग तक
रेंगती है गंध
कैद हवा की।
मैं नहीं जानता

तुम्हें कैसा लगेगा
जब तुम दीवार फाँद कर
भीतर आओगे।

सफ़ेदी पीली पड गई होगी।
अँधेरा कसमसाता
धूल बन जम रहा होगा।

तुम्हारे हाथ
घड़ी की सूइयों को हिलाएँगे
और एक परित्यक्त घोंसला
गिर पड़ेगा तुम्हारे ऊपर।

समय कालीन के नीचे
मरा पड़ा होगा,
चींटियाँ उसे खींच कर
लिए जा रही होंगी।

The doors are closed

The doors are closed
There is no one at home
but memories.

Light slipping through cracks
rises
on the walls
like ribs of silence.

From nostrils to brain
creeps
the smell of prison air.

I don't know
how you'll feel
when you jump over the wall
and come inside.

Whitewash will have turned yellow
wriggling darkness
will be settling into dust.

Your hands
will move those of the clock,
an abandoned nest
will fall on you.

Time will lie dead
under the carpet,
ants will be tugging at it
and carrying it away.

जंगल का दर्द

एक ने मुझे से पूछा :
'जंगल क्या होता है?'
दूसरे ने कहा—'और दर्द?'
मैं ख़ामोश रहा ।

मैंने एक बड़े पिंजड़े में
दोनों को बंद कर दिया
और ऊपर एक काली
झीनी चादर डाल दी ।

कुछ दिनों बाद वे मुझे
जंगली जानवरों की तरह देखने लगे—
पहले उनकी आँखें हरी हुईं
अहिंसक पशुओं जैसी
फिर सुर्ख़, हिंसक पशुओं में बदल गईं
ख़ूँखार –

वे भूखे थे ।
मैंने टुकड़ा फेंका।
वे आहार छोड़
आपस में गूँथ गये,
लहूलुहान हो गये ।

ताकतवर ने सब खा लिया
कमज़ोर ने उच्छिष्ट से
संतोष कर, दर्द से मुँह छिपा लिया ।

यह क्रम बहुत दिनों तक
मैंने बना रहने दिया –
भूखा रखना, टुकड़ा फेंकना,
ताकतवर में दर्प जगाना
और कमज़ोर में संतोष ।

और जब वे
इसके इतने आदी हो गए
कि कुछ और सोच पाना
उनके लिए असम्भव हो गया
तब मैंने उन्हें
पिंजड़े से निकाल दिया ।

अब वे खुले में खड़े थे
खड़े हैं
खड़े रहेंगे
टुकड़े फेंक जाने की प्रतिक्षा में
लड़ने को तैयार
दर्प और संतोष के
      शिकार ।

The pain of the jungle

The first asked me:
'What is a jungle?'
the second added–'And pain?'
I remained silent.

I locked them both
in a big cage
and covered it
with a worn black sheet.

After a few days they
were looking at me like wild animals–

First their eyes were green
like those of gentle creatures
then red, turning them into beasts of prey,
bloodthirsty–

They were hungry.
I threw them a scrap.
They left the food
their bodies tangled,
smeared with blood.

The strong ate most of it
the weak, resigned to the leftovers,
pained, hid his face.

For many days
I followed this sequence–
keeping them hungry, throwing them a scrap,
arousing arrogance in the strong
and resignation in the weak.

And when they
were so used to that
that they could not
think about anything else
I let them
out of the cage.

They were standing in the open space,
are standing,
will be standing
Waiting for a scrap to be thrown
Ready to fight
    Prey
to arrogance and resignation.

कुआनो नदी

. . .

कुआनो नदी वैसी ही पसरी रहती है
हर समय मेरी आँखों के सामने।

बहुत गरीब ज़िला है वह, बस्ती –
जहाँ मैंने इसे पहली बार देखा था।
मेरे नाना इस नदी में कूद पड़े थे
और निकाल लिये गये थे
ज़िन्दगी से ऊब कर मर नहीं सके।
तट पर न रेत थी न सीपियाँ
सख़्त कँकरीली ज़मीन थी काई लगी,
कहीं–कहीं दलदल था, झाड़ियाँ थीं दूर तक
जिनमें साँप कुलबुलाते रहते थे
और चिड़ियाँ एक टहनी से दूसरी टहनी पर
शोर करती झूलती रहती थीं।

यह नदी मुर्दघाट के लिए मशहूर है।
कुआनो जाने का मतलब
किसी को फूँकने जाना है।
मेरे पिता को हर शिव-यात्रा में जाने का शोक था।
अक्सर वह आधी-आधी रात लौटते
और लकड़ियाँ गीली होने की शिकायत करते।
माँ से कहते – 'कुछ लोग अभागे होते हैं
उनकी चिता ठीक से नहीं जलती'
और हर अभागे की यही आख़िरी कहानी
मैं आज भी सुनता हूँ।

इस नदी के किनारे
कोई मेला नहीं लगता।
नहीं पूर्णिमा-स्नान होते हैं।
एक मंदिर है
जो बहुत कम खुलता है
जिसकी सीढ़ियाँ
अहदियों के बैठने के काम आती हैं।
मैं अक्सर वहाँ बैठा रहता हूँ
और दालान के कोने में
टूटा, जाला लगा चमड़े का
एक बहुत पुराना बड़ा ढोल टँगा
देखता रहता हूँ जो अब बजता नहीं
और तेज़ हवा में
खड़खड़ाते विशाल झीने पीपल के पेड़ से
देवी स्पर्श की तरह
किसी जालीदार पीले पत्ते के अपने ऊपर

गिरने की प्रतीक्षा करता रहता हूँ।

. . .

धूप में शहर की गंदगी
यहाँ साफ होती है
धोबी कपडे धोते हैं,
आवारा औरतें सिगरेट पीती
गुनगुनाती-लिपटती
अपने ग्राहकों के साथ घूमती हैं।
रात में अक्सर कत्ल होते हैं।
लाशें कई-कई दिनों की पायी जाती हैं।
किसी स्त्री का फेंका हुआ
नया जन्मा बच्चा
कभी ज़िन्दा कभी मरा मिल जाता है।
शाम होते ही पुलिस
भारी टार्चों से रोशनी फेंकती
पुल पर गश्त लगाती है
और सियार हुआँ-हुआँ करते हैं।
चमगादड़ों के उड़ने से
शाखें खड़खड़ाती हैं
और कि सी अकेली चिता की
आख़िरी लपटें, बड़े-बड़े दहकते
अंगारों की आँखों से देखती हैं,
ऊपर आसमान में तारे होते हैं
नीचे नदी चुपचाप बहती जाती है।

The Kuano river[3]

. . .

The Kuano river, unchanged, stretches
before my eyes all the time.

It's a desperately poor district, Basti–
where I saw it for the first time.
My grandfather jumped into that river
and was pulled out,
weary of life, he couldn't die.
On the bank there was neither sand, nor shells
but hard, stony earth, covered with scum.
There were marshes here and there, undergrowth into the distance,
in which streams were restless
and noisy birds swung
from one twig to the next.

...

This river is famous for its burning ghat.
To go to Kuano means
to go to burn someone.
My father liked going to every funeral procession.
Often he would come at midnight
and complain about the wood being damp.
He would say to mother, 'Some people are unfortunate
their pyres don't burn properly'–
I can still hear
that last story of every unfortunate.

There is never a fair
on the banks of this river.
Nobody bathes there at full moon.
There is a temple
which is rarely open,
its steps are used by idlers to sit.
I often sit there
and keep looking at an old, big drum,
hanging in a corner of the hallway,
broken, the skin covered in cobwebs,
it resounds no more.
And in the strong wind
I keep waiting for
a netted yellow leaf to fall on me
from the rustling, huge, worn-out pipal tree
like a divine touch.

...

The town's dirt
is cleaned here in the sunlight,
Washermen wash clothes,
Stray women smoke cigarettes,
walk, humming and clinging to their customers.
Murders happen often at night
days-old corpses are discovered.
Some woman's discarded
newly-born
is found sometimes alive, sometimes dead.
When evening comes the police
keep guard on the bridge
casting light with big torches

and jackals howl.
Branches rustle
with flying bats
and the last flames of a lonely pyre
watch with the eyes of huge burning cinders.
There are stars in the sky above.
Below the river flows on silently.

Notes and References

[1]   The places described in this poem hold special significance for Saxena, since they mark important points in his life: born in Basti, he was educated in Benares and Allahabad and died in Delhi. However, Delhi, Lucknow, Benares and Allahabad are also cultural symbols of wider relevance, and Saxena has managed to capture the spirit of these cities with a few well-chosen details: the sense of transience, of the uneasy mix of refined Muslim culture and its pragmatic, money-oriented capitalist successor represented by Delhi; the past glory of the once elegant and sophisticated nawabi culture in Lucknow; the ancient history and religious air of Benares, enhanced by a rather liberal use of *bhāg* (cannabis) and Allahabad's association with both the Ganges, on which it is situated, and the 'coffee-house culture', popular with the Hindi intelligentsia in the mid-20th century.

[2]   This is the text of the poem as published in Shukla 1996. In Saxena 1966 (pp. 16–17) 'Rain at night' includes three more stanzas.

[3]   Saxena has dedicated a whole collection of poems to Kuano, the river of his childhood. The book is represented here by extracts from 'The Kuano river', a poem which runs over seven pages in the edition I have used. It is a collage of images, together creating the powerful symbol of the river, a witness to the tragic existence of the poor.

In the huge carnival of life the poet is like a mimic who presents to people thousands of appearances. His every appearance is an experiential interpretation of life and behind them all is the mimic's thoughtful true personality which understands the fundamental play of all this diversity.

(Kunwar Narain in Agyeya 1996c, p.157)

Kunwar Narain
B. 1927

This image of the poet, with its complexity, thoughtfulness and erudition (the 'carnival' of life suggesting a familiarity with the works of Bakhtin) gives us a sense of Kunwar Narain's creative persona. He is a true intellectual, 'one of the most well-read poets in Hindi' (Bhardwaj 1998, p.1). Kunwar Narain's volume of interviews *Mere sākṣātkār* testifies to his remarkable familiarity with the cultural achievements of mankind: he speaks with equal ease (and with plentiful quotations from impressively varied sources) about European poetry, schools of literary criticism, mythology, philosophy, film studies, art, theatre, Indian classical music, translation, etc. etc. And yet his encyclopaedic knowledge is never paraded. Kunwar Narain is interested in ideas, not because they are the Truth, but because they can be the 'means to reaching another truth' (Agyeya 1996c, p.155). In his statement in *Tīsrā saptak* Kunwar Narain makes clear that 'the scientific point of view', which he considers essential to any writer, is 'not the theories of Marx, Freud, Einstein, Newton or Darwin, but the intellectual freedom that always raises fearless and examining questions concerning life', 'a tolerant and neutral mental disposition which does not lame life with pre-conceived ideas, but approaches it with logic and alertness' (ibid., pp.155, 154)

It is the 'battle between an erudite, refined brain and a sensitive, intensely emotional heart' (Rav 1965, p.27), Kunwar Narain's unique 'poised vulnerability' (Shah 1994, p.7), which has tuned the deep humanistic voice of his writing. His poetry is crafted with conscious effort, experimentation and relentless editing. It employs myth and tradition, but it takes nothing for granted: everything is re-examined, the poet is 'a neutral and detached thinker-investigator'. (Rav 1965, p.31) Even the poetical work itself has to be re-examined, to be tested against time: Kunwar Narain never rushes to publish, he patiently edits and re-edits.

His poems are typically very dense; they demand a conscious effort from the reader. Every reading discloses a new layer, a different pattern in the intricate design of the whole. Therefore it is not surprising that Kunwar Narain's poetry has sometimes been criticised for being obscure and inaccessible. It is certainly complex, multi-faceted, revealing 'a 20th century sensibility in its anguish as well as its resourcefulness'. (Shah 1994, p.1)

What has shaped Kunwar Narain's creative persona? Born in Faizabad (UP) in 1927, he spent his early childhood there and in Ayodhya. When he was eleven both his mother and his sister died of tuberculosis. The shock of this enormous loss and concerns regarding his own health made death a recurrent theme in Kunwar Narain's poetry. It is not by chance that his long narrative poem *Ātmajayī* (The conquest of the self) is a meditation on death, 'a myth against the despair death brings' (Bhardwaj 1998, p.1).

After this family tragedy Kunwar Narain moved to Lucknow, then a major cultural centre, famous for its thriving university and its legendary Coffee House. He did a course in science, followed by an MA in English (Raghuvir Sahay being his fellow student), and frequented the Coffee House, which acted as a magnet for intellectuals in North India.

Kunwar Narain spent a year with the socialist politician Acharya Narendra Dev in Bombay, which exposed him not only to literature and philosophy (Marxism and Buddhism in particular), but also to the reality of Indian politics. In 1954 he stayed with Acharya Kripalani in Delhi and worked as an assistant to the editor of *Vigil*. He has also edited other magazines, among them *Yugcetnā* and *Nayā Pratīk*, but most of his time has been devoted to creative writing, film, music and theatre. Kunwar Narain's deep engagement with the last two is reflected by the positions of Vice-President of the UP Sangeet Natak Academy and President of Bharatendu Natya Academy, which he held in the 1970s. His well-to-do business family allowed him to pursue his interests despite their initial disappointment and reluctance. In his own joking words: 'they considered me to be the "spare part" of the family and spared me to do my reading and writing' (Bhardwaj 1999, p.24).

Like Agyeya, Kunwar Narain is a traveller: he has visited many countries of Eastern and Western Europe, China and the USA, and lectured in a number of them. He has published five collections of verse and the long narrative poem *Ātmajayī* and contributed to Agyeya's *Tīsrā saptak*. He has also written short stories, literary criticism and plays, and has translated Cavafy and Borges from English into Hindi. His many honours include the prestigious Hindustani Akademi and the Sahitya Akademi awards.

Kunwar Narain does not see reality through rose-tinted glasses. He is not afraid of scrutinizing the past and present with an awareness of his responsibility to the future. He acknowledges man's greatness and fallibility with honesty and compassion. It would not do justice to his poetry to try to fit it into any formula, and yet if we have to characterise it with one word, it must be humanism–Kunwar Narain's poetry teaches us not to forget our duty to remain human.

The text of the poems is from Narain 1989a, 1989b, 1996 and Bhardwaj 1999. Bhardwaj 1999 is an extremely informative collection of Kunwar Narain's interviews. His poetry has been translated in: Mishra 1967, pp.66 and 99; Weissbort 1993, pp.81–5; Weissbort 1994, pp.10–19; Dharwadker 1996, p.159; Vajpeyi 1998, pp.64–72; Ramakrishnan 1999, pp.183–6; Satchidanandan 2000, pp.147–51 *Indian horizons*, vol. 42, pp.51–6; and *Indian literature* 153, pp.35–9.

Kunwar   Narain

कमरे में धूप

हवा और दरवाज़ों में बहस होती रही,
दीवारें सुनती रहीं।
धूप चुपचाप एक कुरसी पर बैठी
किरणों के ऊन का स्वेटर बुनती रही।

सहसा किसी बात पर बिगड़ कर
हवा ने दरवाज़े को तड़ से
एक थप्पड़ जड़ दिया!

खिड़कियाँ गरज उठीं,

अख़बार उठ कर खड़ा हो गया,
किताबें मुँह बाये देखती रहीं,
पानी से भरी सुराही फ़र्श पर टूट पड़ी,
मेज़ के हाथ से क़लम छूट पड़ी।

धूप उठी और बिना कुछ कहे
कमरे से बाहर चली गई।

शाम को लौटी तो देखा
एक कुहराम के बाद घर में ख़ामोशी थी।
अँगड़ाई लेकर पलंग पर पड़ गई,
पड़े-पड़े कुछ सोचती रही,
सोचते सोचते न जाने कब सो गई,
आँख खुली तो देखा सुबह हो गई।

Sunlight in the room

The wind argued with the doors,
the walls listened.
Sunlight sat on a chair, quietly
knitting a sweater of ray-wool.

Suddenly the wind
grew angry,
slapped the door with a bang!

The windows roared,
the newspaper stood up,
the books stared, agape,
the jug full of water hit the floor,
the table dropped the pen.

Sunlight rose and left the room
without a word.

She returned in the evening,
the house was calm after the storm.
She stretched on the bed,
brooding for a long time
and fell asleep.
It was morning when she woke up.

अंतिम ऊँचाई

कित्ना स्पष्ट होता आगे बढ़ते जाने का मतलब
अगर दसों दिशाएँ हमारे सामने होतीं,
       हमारे चारों ओर नही।
कित्ना आसान होता चलते चले जाना
यदि केवल हम चलते होते
       बाक़ी सब रुका होता।
मैंने अक्सर इक ऊलजलूल दुनिया को
दस सिरों से सोचने और बीस हाथों से पाने की कोशिश में
अपने लिए बेहद मुश्किल बना लिया है।
शुरू–शुरू में सब यही चाहते हैं
कि सब कुछ शुरू से शुरू हो,
लेकिन अन्त तक पहुँचते –पहुँचते हिम्मत हार जाते हैं।
हमें कोई दिलचस्पी नही रहती
कि वह सब कैसे समास होता है
जो इतनी धूमधाम से शुरू हुआ था
       हमारे चाहने पर।
दुर्गम बनों और ऊंचे पर्वतों को जीतते हुए
जब तुम अन्तिम ऊँचाई को भी जीत लोगे–
जब तुम्हें लगेगा कि कोई अन्तर नही बचा अब
तुममें और उन पत्थरों को कठोरता में
       जिन्हें तुमने जीता है–
जब तुम अपने मस्तक पर बर्फ़ का पहला तूफ़ान झेलोगे
       और काँपोगे नहीं –
अब तुम पाओगे कि कोई फ़र्क़ नहीं
सब कुछ जीत लेने में
और अंन्त तक हिम्मत न हारने में।

The last ascent

How clear the meaning of going forward would be
if all[1] directions were in front of us,
    not around us.
How easy moving on would be

if only we were moving
  all the rest was still.
I've often made it endlessly difficult for myself
trying to think with ten heads and take with twenty hands
this absurd world.
In the beginning everybody wants
everything to begin from the beginning,
but as we reach the end we lose heart.
We don't care any more
how all this will end
that had begun with such ostentation
  at our wish.
When you conquer the last ascent,
defeating dense jungles and high mountains–
When it seems to you that no difference remains
between you and the harshness of the stones
  that you have conquered–
When you endure the first snowstorm on your head
  without trembling–
You'll know, then, that there is no difference
between conquering everything
and not losing courage till the end.

बाक़ी कविता
पत्तों पर पानी गिरने का अर्थ
पानी पर पत्ते गिरने के अर्थ से भिन्न है ।

जीवन को पूरी तरह पाने
और पूरी तरह दे जाने के बीच
एक पूरा मृत्यु-चिह्न है ।

बाक़ी कविता
शब्दों से नहीं लिखी जाती,
पूरे अस्तित्व को खींचकर एक विराम की तरह
कहीं भी छोड़ दी जाती है. . .

The rest of the poem

Water falling on leaves means one thing
Leaves falling on water another.

Between gaining life fully
and giving it away fully
stands a full death-mark.

The rest of the poem

is written not with words—
Drawing the whole of existence, like a full stop,
it is complete at any point . . .

दूर तक

अँधेरे को अचानक फूल बनाती हुई सुगंध
सुगंध को रूप देते हुए रंग
रंगों को एक चमक देता हुआ मौसम
मौसम को गोद देती हुई ज़मीन
ज़मीन को भर देते हुए बादल
बादल को आकाश देती हुई हवा. . .
　　आओ इन सबको अपने में भरकर
　　दूर तक फैल जायें. . .

Reaching out

Fragrance turning darkness into flower,
Colours giving form to the fragrance,
Seasons giving a glow to the colours,
Earth giving her bosom to the seasons,
Clouds giving fulfilment to the earth,
Breeze giving sky to the clouds . . .
　　Come, let's take all this in
　　and reach out a long way . . .

एक संक्षिप्त कालखण्ड में

अगर मुझमें अपनी दुनिया को
बदल सकने की ताक़त होती
तो सब से पहले
उस 'मैं' को बदलने से शुरू करता
जिसमें दुनिया को बदल ने की ताक़त होती।

उसे एक पिचका गुब्बारा देता
जिस पर दुनिया का नक़्शा बना होता।
और कहता–
　　इसमें अपनी साँसे भरो,
　　इसे फुला कर
　　अपने से करोडों गुना बडा कर लो,
　　और फिर अनुभव करो
　　कि तुम उत्ना ही उसके अन्दर हो
　　जितना उसके बाहर
धीरे धीरे एक असह्य दबाव में
बदलती चली जाएगी
तुम्हारे प्रयत्नों की भूमिका,

किसी अन्य यथार्थ में प्रवेश कर जाने को
बेचैन हो उठेंगी तुम्हारी चिन्ताएँ।
उससे कहता–
एक हिम्मत और करो,
अपनी पूरी ताक़त लगा कर
ग़ुब्बारे को थोडा और फुलाओ
. . . लगभग . . . फूटने की हद तक . . .
अब देखो कि तुम
इस कोशिश में
नष्ट हो जाते हो
एक कर्कश विस्फोट के साथ
या किसी विरल ऊँचाई को
छू पाता है तुम्हारा गुब्बारा
हवा से भी हल्का
और कल्पना की तरह मुक्त

In a brief span of time

If I could change
the world
first
I would change that 'I'
who could change the world.
I would give him a deflated balloon,
with the map of the world,
and say–
'Fill it with your breath,
blow it full,
make it a million times bigger than you,
and feel
that you are inside it,
as much as outside.'
Slowly the unbearable strain
will change the nature of your efforts,
your concerns will struggle to enter
a different realm of reality.
'Dare now', I would say,
'Give it all you have
and blow the balloon yet bigger
almost to bursting point . . .

Now see–
Either this effort

will destroy you
with a violent blast

Or your balloon
will touch some rare height
lighter than air,
freer than fantasy.'

कबूतर ओर बिल्ली
उस तस्वीर में
सब से ऊँचे कंगूरे पर बैठा कबूतर
        मान लें ज़िन्दा है
और तस्वीर के बाहर
कहीं अँधेरों में दुबकी बिल्ली
        उस पर झपटने ही वाली है।

एक पंजा अगर बिल्ली को दबोच ले
तो उस की म्याँऊँ टें में बदल जायेगी

तेज़ हवा में
तस्वीर वाला कबूतर
फडफडा कर उड जायेगा।
कबूतर अगर उड सके
तो आज़ाद होगा तस्वीर की कैद से
बिल्ली अगर झपट पाये
तो कैद होगी तस्वीर के पिंजरे में।
उड सकने और झपट लेने के बीच
जो फ़र्क हैं
तस्वीर से ज़रा दूर हटने पर
साफ़ दिखाई देता है।

Pigeon and cat

Imagine that
the pigeon on the high parapet
in this picture
    is alive.

And that a cat, crouching
in the darkness outside the picture
    is about to pounce upon the bird.

If a claw seizes the cat,
its meowing will become a screech.

The pigeon in the picture
will flutter its wings and fly away
in the swift air.

If the pigeon could fly
it would be free of the picture's prison,
if the cat could pounce
it would be imprisoned in the picture's cage.

The difference
between flying and pouncing
can be seen clearly
if you step back a little.

बदलते पोस्टर

एक ढहती दीवार पर
नये नये ख़ुशरंग पोस्टर
पुराने पड़ने से पहले
बदलते रहते हैं अकसर

कभी लि रिल साबुन में नहाती सुन्दरी,
कभी डालडा वनस्पति से पनपते बच्चे,
कभी इफ़को ख़ाद से लहलहाती फ़सलें,
कभी सदाबहार पान के मसाले,
कभी ऐटलस साइकिल परसवार पग्गड़ किसान,
कभी हाथ जोड़े खड़े धनवर्षा का संदेश देते
        धनकुबेर ।
मगर वह गुमसुम उदास लड़का नहीं बदलता
जो ठीक पर सरकारी पोसटर लगाता है –
    'बाप शराब पियेंगे
    और बेटे भूखों मरेंगे . . .'

Changing posters

On a shabby wall
new, colourful posters
keep on changing
before they grow old

Sometimes a beauty bathing in 'Liril' soap,
Sometimes children thriving on 'Dalda' oil,
Sometimes 'IFFCO' fertiliser promising a rich harvest,
Sometimes 'Sadabahar' betel-spices,
Sometimes a turbaned villager on an 'Atlas' bike,
Sometimes a god of wealth with folded hands
announcing a rain of gold!

But what never changes
is that sad, quiet boy
who puts up official posters for a pittance—

'When father drinks
the children starve . . .'

प्रेम का रोग

एक अजीब-सी मुशिकल में हूँ इन दिनों
मेरी भरपूर नफ़रत कर सकने की ताकत
दिनोंदिन क्षीण पडती जा रही !

अंग्रजी से नफ़रता करना चाहता
(जिन्होंने दो सदी हम पर राज किया)
तो शेक्सपियर आड़े आज जाते
जिनके मुझ पर न जाने कित्ने एहसान हैं ।

मुसलमानों से नफ़रत करने चलता
तो सामने गालिब आ कर खड़े हो जाते ।
अब आप ही बताइए – किसकी कुछ चलती है
उनके सामने ?

सिखों से नफ़रत करना चाहता
तो गुरू नानक आँखों में छा जाते
और सिर अपने आप झुक जाता

और ये कंबन, त्यागराज, मुत्तुस्वामी . . .
लाख समझाता अपने को
कि ये मेरे नहीं
दूर कहीं दक्षिण के हैं
पर मन है कि मानता ही नहीं
बिना इन्हें अपनाए

और वह प्रेमिका
जिस्से मुझे पहला धोखा हुआ था
मिल जाए तो उसका खून कर दूँ!
मिलता भी है, मगर
कभी मित्र
कभी माँ
कभी बहन की तरह
तो प्यार का घूँट पीकर रह जाता !

हर समय
पागलों की तरह भटकता रहता
कि कहीं कोई ऐसा मिल जाए
जिस्से भरपूर नफ़रत कर के
अपना जी हलका कर लूँ!

पर होता है इसका ठीक उल्टा
कोई-न-कोई, कहीं-न-कहीं, कभी-न-कभी,
ऐसा मिल जाता
जिस्से प्यार किए बिना रह ही नहीं पाता ।

दिनोंदिन मेरा यह प्रेम-रोग बढ़ता ही जा रहा
और इस वहम ने पक्की जड पकड़ ली है
कि यह प्रेम किसी दिन मुझे
स्वर्ग दिखा कर ही रहेगा ।

Day by day[2]

I've a strange problem these days–
    my ability to hate with passion
    is failing me day by day.

I want to hate the English
    (who ruled us for two centuries)
    but Shakespeare gets in the way
    He's done so much for me!

I try to hate the Muslims
    but Ghalib[3] intervenes
    You tell me–can anyone
    disregard him?

I want to hate the Sikhs
    but Guru Nanak appears
    and my head bows of its own accord.

And these Kamban, Tyagaraja, Muttusvami . . .
    I keep telling myself–
    They are not mine,
    they are of the far South
    But my heart doesn't listen
    and makes them its own.

And that woman I once loved
    who deceived me . . .
    I could kill her if I met her!
    We do meet, but then
    the friend in her,
    or the mother, or the sister
    nourish me with love.

All the time
    I wander like a madman
    looking for someone
    I could hate to my heart's content
    and feel light!

But the opposite happens
    sometime, somewhere
    I always meet someone

whom I cannot but love!

Day by day this love-sickness is growing
  and the suspicion has gripped me
  that one day this love
  will send me to heaven . . .

Notes and References

[1] The original 'ten (directions)' is an oblique reference to Ravana, the ten-headed demon of the *Rāmȳana*. Perhaps more obvious to the European reader is a parallel between the last stanza of this poem and Kipling's popular 'If'.

[2] This title is suggested by the poet.

[3] Ghalib (1797–1869) was arguably the most famous poet of Persian and Urdu in India. Guru Nanak (1469–1539) is venerated as the founder of Sikhism. The 9th-century poet Kamban is known for composing *Irāmāvatāram*, a Tamil version of the *Rāmāyana*. Muttuswami Dikshitar and Tyagaraja, two of the most prominent Carnatic musicians, lived in the late 18th and early 19th centuries.

Kedarnath Singh
B. 1934

Kedarnath Singh grew up in the village of Chakia (UP), in a house 'between the Ganges and the river Ghaghra'. His childhood as a peasant boy, surrounded by nature, moulded his poetic sensibility. 'Somewhere inside me the waves of the Ganges and Ghaghra constantly collide. The imprint on my heart of vast low lands, maize fields and paths reaching into the distance is still as strong as it was on the day when I first came under the smoky, fragmented sky of the city.' (Agyeya 1996c, p.122) Kedarnath Singh's words point to another presence in his poetic world: the city, to which he came to study–he did an MA and a PhD in Hindi Literature at Benares Hindu University; and to work–he taught at various colleges in Benares, Gorakhpur, Pandrauma, and he presently lectures at Jawaharlal Nehru University in New Delhi.

The exposure to village and city life has created the breadth of Kedarnath Singh's experience. The village and the city are present not only as subject matter in his poetry but also as the source of images. This is demonstrated by the selection of his poems in the present anthology: whereas in 'I saw the Ganges' nature is one of the protagonists–the Ganges is a source of livelihood and inner peace for the old boatman–in 'Come' nature is used simply to contribute to the richness of imagery.

Imagery is central to Kedarnath Singh's poetry. It is not by chance that he wrote his doctoral thesis on the creation of images in contemporary Hindi poetry. He believes that images have replaced characters in contemporary poetry. (ibid., p.123) Nature is probably the most important source of his imagery but certainly not the only one: folk-tales, religion, science and traditional scriptures also add colour to his rich poetical canvas. For example the poem 'Tiger 6' is part of a book-long cycle of poems which explores the complex reality of contemporary life through the composite image of the tiger, an image in which nature is informed by the traditional fables of The Pañcatantra.

Kedarnath Singh has published seven collections of poems apart from his contribution to Agyeya's Tīsrā saptak. Throughout his development as a poet his verses have remained closely connected with everyday life. There is nothing he sees as unsuitable for poetry: a kitchen knife, a spade, a broken truck–all find place in his verses. As he himself asserts:

There is no limit to the subject matter of poetry. There are some themes
which find expression in every age: birth, death, nature, the seasons.
Parallel to them there is the dynamic cycle of life in which the daily joys
and sorrows of the world, hopes and ambitions, the rise and fall of cultures,
the creation and destruction of cities, the celebration of harvests keep
turning. The place of a poet is amidst those.

(Agyeya 1996c, p.124).

The everyday-life subject matter of his poetry is matched by the simplicity
of his language. His verses carry the rhythm of daily existence, often the simple
tonality of folk songs. Kedarnath lists 'poetry, music and solitude' as the 'three
things extremely dear to me'. (ibid., p.121) Though he has written literary
criticism and essays, he is first and foremost a poet. Thanks to the accessibility
of his language and subject matter, he is currently one of the most popular
Hindi poets. He has been given many honours, including the prestigious Sahitya
Akademi Award. His poetry has been translated into most major Indian and
European languages.

'I always try to keep my heart open so that it can echo the slightest sound of
life around me', says Kedarnath Singh in his statement in *Tīsrā saptak* (ibid.,
p.125). It is this open heart, a heart which pulsates with old boatmen and
playing children, shepherds and poets, spades and kitchen knives, rivers and
mountains, bullocks and birds, bread and salt, the sun and the earth, that gives
his poetry a rich, lasting resonance.

The text of the poems is from Shrivastav 1993, Singh 1990, 1995a, 1995b
and 1996. Kedarnath Singh's poetry has been translated in Misra 1967, pp.46–
7, 54, 91, 106–7, 115; Weissbort 1994, pp.20–31; Dharwadkar 1996, pp.4–6;
Vajpeyi 1998, pp.109–21; Ramakrishnan 1999, pp.171–82, Satchidanandan
2000, pp.236–41; *Indian Horizons* vol. 42, pp.62–5 and *Indian literature* 153,
pp.19–34. Munshi 1996 is a translation of the Sahitya Academy Award winning
Akāl mē̃ sāras. Indian literature 153 contains an informative interview with
Kedarnath Singh (pp.123–40).

Kedarnath Singh

बाज़ार

'आओ बाज़ार चलें'
उसने कहा
'बाजार में क्या है' ?
मैंने पूछा
'बाजार में धूल है'
उसने हँसते हुए कहा ।

एक अजीब-सी मिट्टी की चमक
उसके हँसने में थी
जो मुझे अच्छी लगी
मैंने पूछा-धूल !
'धूल में क्या है' ?
'जनता'-उसने बेहद सादगी से कहा ।

मैं कुछ देर स्तब्ध खड़ा रहा
फिर हम दोनों चल पड़े
धूल और जनता की तलाश में
वहाँ पहुँचकर
हमें आश्चर्य हुआ
बाज़ार में न धूल थी
न जनता
दोनों को साफ़ कर दिया गया था

Market

'Come, let's go to the market',
he said.
'What's there?',
I asked.
'Dust',
He laughed.
There was a strange earthy sparkle
in his laugh
which I liked

I asked–'Dust!
What's in the dust?'
'People'–he said simply.

I stood stunned for a while
Then we set off
in search of dust and people
When we got there
we were amazed–
Neither dust nor people
were in the market

Both had been cleaned out.

अकाल में सारस

तीन बजे दिन में
आ गये वे
जब वे आये
किसी ने सोचा तक नहीं था
कि ऐसे भी आ सकते हैं सारस

एक के बाद एक
वे झुंड के झुंड
धीरे-धीरे आये
धीरे-धीरे वे छा गये
सारे आसमान में
धीरे-धीरे उनके ट्रेंकार से भर गया
सारा का सारा शहर

वे देर तक करते रहे
शहर की परिक्रमा
देर तक छतों और बारजों पर
उनके डैनों से झरती रही
धान की सूखी
पत्तियों की गंध

अचानक
एक बुढ़िया ने उन्हें देखा
ज़रूर ज़रूर
वे पानी की तलाश में आये हैं
उसने सोचा

वह रसोई में गई
और आँगन के बीचोबीच
लाकर रख दिया
एक जलभरा कटोरा

लेकिन सारस
उसी तरह करते रहे
शहर की परिक्रमा

न तो उन्होंने बुढ़िया को देखा
न जलभर कटोरे को

सारसों को तो पता तक नहीं था
कि नीचे रहते हैं लोग
जो उन्हें कहते हैं सारस
पानी को खोजते
दूर-देसावर से आये थे वे
पानी को खोजते
दूर-देसावर तक जाना था उन्हें
सो, उन्होंने गर्दन उठाई
एक बार पीछे की ओर देखा
न जाने क्या था उस निगाह में
दया कि घृणा
पर एक बार जाते-जाते
उन्होंने शहर की ओर मुंडकर
देखा ज़रूर

फिर हवा में
अपने डैन पीटते हुए
दूरियों में धीरे-धीरे
खो गये सारस।

Cranes in the drought

They came
at three o'clock in the afternoon
When they came
nobody had even thought
that cranes could come like this

One by one,
flock after flock,
they came slowly
Slowly they covered
the entire sky
Slowly their cries filled
the entire town

For a long time
they circled above the town
For a long time the smell
of rice plant's dry leaves
kept falling from their wings
onto roofs and porches

Suddenly
an old woman saw them
and thought–
For certain
they have come in search of water
She went into the kitchen,
brought out a bowl of water
and left it
in the middle of the courtyard

But the cranes
kept circling in the same way
above the town
they saw neither the old woman
nor the bowl of water

They didn't even know
that down there lived people
who called them cranes

In search of water
they had come from faraway lands

In search of water
they had to go on to faraway lands

So they raised their necks,
looked back once more

Who knows what was in this glance–
compassion or aversion
They certainly looked once
back towards the town
as they were leaving

Then beating their wings
in the air
slowly the cranes disappeared
in the distance

आना

आना
जब समय मिले
जब समय न मिले
तब भी आना

आना
जैसे हाथों में

आता है जाँगर
जैसे धमनियों में
आता है रक्त
जैसे चूल्हों में
धीरे-धीरे आती है आँच
आना
आना जैसे बारिश के बाद
बबूल में आ जाते हैं
नये-नये काँटे

दिनों को
चीरते-फाडते
और वादों की धज्जियाँ उडाते हुए
आना

आना जैसे मंगल के बाद
चला आता है बुध
आना

Come

Come
when you have time
when you don't have time
come even then

Come
as vigour comes
into the hands,
as blood comes
into the veins,
as fire slowly comes
into the stoves
Come

Come
as new thorns come
into the acacia
after rain

Shattering days,
tearing promises to shreds
Come

Come
as Wednesday
comes along after Tuesday
Come

कुछ और टुकड़े
(१)
अकेली चुप्पी
भयानक चीज़ है
जैसे हवा में गैंडे का
अकेला सींग

पर यदि दो लोग चुप हों
पास-पास बैठे हुए
तो उतनी देर
भाषा के गर्भ में
चुपचाप बनती रहती है
एक और भाषा

Some more fragments[1]

[I]
Solitary silence
is a fearsome thing
like a rhinoceros' solitary horn
in the air

But if two people are silent,
sitting side by side
In that short while
from language's womb
silently rises
a new language

सुखी आदमी
आज वह रोया
यह सोचते हुए कि रोना
कितना हास्यास्पद है
वह रोया

मौसम अच्छा था
धूप खिली हुई
सब ठीक-ठाक
सब दुरूस्त
बस खिड़की खोलते ही
सलाख़ों से दिख गया
ज़रा-सा आसमान
और वह रोया

फूटकर नहीं

जैसे जानवर रोता है माँद में
वह रोया।

A happy man

Today he cried,
thinking
how ridiculous crying is,
he cried

The weather was nice,
the sun radiant
All fine
All healthy
Only as he opened the window
a bit of sky
showed through the bars
and he cried

Not bitterly
Like an animal crying in its lair,
he cried.

बाघ ६

'ये आदमी लोग
इतने चुप क्यों रहते हैं आजकल ?'–
एक दिन बाघ ने लोमडी से पूछा
लोमडी की समझ में कुछ नही आया
पर उसने समर्थन में सिर हिलाया
और एकटक देखती रही बाघ के जबड़ों को
जिनसे अब भी ताज़ा ख़ून को गंध आ रही थी
फिर कुछ दरे बाद कुछ सोचते हुए बोली–
'कोई दुख होगा उन्हें'

'कैसा दुख ?'
बाघ ने तड़पकर पूछा
'यह में नहीं जानती
पर दुख का क्या
वह हो ही जाता है कैसे भी'
लोमडी ने उत्तर दिया

'हो सकता है
उन्हें कोई काँटा गडा हो ?' बाघ ने पूछा

'हो सकता है
पर हो सकता है आदमी ही
गड गया हो काँटे को'

लोमडी ने धीरे से कहा
अबकी बाघ की समझ में
कुछ नहीं आया
पर उसने समर्थन में

उसी तरह सिर हिलाया
फिर धीरे से पूछा–
'क्या आदमी लोग
पानी पीते हैं ?'

'पीते हैं '–लोमडी ने कहा–
'पर वे हमारी तरह
सिर्फ सुबह–शाम नहीं पीते,
दिन–भर में जितनी बार चाहा
उतनी बार पीते हैं '

'पर इतना पानी क्यों पीते हैं
आदमी लोग ?'
बाघ ने आश्चर्य से पूछा

'वही दुख–
मैंने कहा न !'
लोमडी ने उत्तर दिया

इस बार फिर
बाघ की समझ में कुछ नहीं आया
पर वह देर तक सिर झुकाए
उसी तरह सोचता रहा

यह 'दुख' एक ऐसा शब्द था
जिसके सामने बाघ
बिलकुल निरूपाय था ।

The Tiger[2]

'Why are these humans
so quiet nowadays?' –
one day the tiger asked the fox
The fox understood nothing,
but nodded in agreement
and kept staring at the tiger's jaws
which still smelled of fresh blood
Then she thought for a while and said–
'They must have some sorrow'

'What sorrow?',
the tiger asked eagerly
'I don't know,

but sorrow is sorrow—
it always comes somehow',
the fox replied

'Maybe
a thorn has pierced them?', the tiger asked

'Maybe
but maybe man
has pierced the thorn',
the fox said slowly.
This time the tiger
understood nothing,
but nodded in agreement
Then he asked slowly,
'Do humans
drink water?'

'They do'–the fox said–
'but not only in the morning and evening
as we do,
they drink all day long
as often as they want'

'But why do humans drink
so much water?',
the tiger was surprised

'I've already told you—
because of sorrow!',
the fox answered

Once again
the tiger understood nothing,
but he kept thinking for a long time
his head bent

'Sorrow' was a word
before which the tiger
was totally helpless

मैंने गंगा को देखा

मैंने गंगा को देखा
एक लम्बे सफर के बाद
जब मेरी आँखें
कुछ भी देखने को तरस रही थीं
जब मेरे पास कोई काम नहीं था

मैंने गंगा को देखा
प्रचंड लू के थपेड़ों के बाद
जब एक शाम
मुझे साहस और ताज़गी की
बेहद ज़रूरत थी
मैंने गंगा को देखा एक रोहू मछली थी
डब-डब आँख में
जहाँ जीने की अपार तरलता थी
मैंने गंगा को देखा जहां एक बूढ़ा मल्लाह
रेती पर खड़ा था
घर जाने को तैयार
और मैंने देखा –
बूढ़ा खुश था
वर्ष के उन सबसे उदास दिनों में भी
मैं हैरान रह गया यह देखकर
कि गंगा के जल में कितनी लम्बी
और शानदार लगती है
एक बूढ़े आदमी के खुश होने के परछाई !

अब बूढ़ा ज़रा हिला
उसने अपना जाल उठाया
कंधे पर रखा
चलने से पहले
एक बार फिर गंगा की ओर देखा
और मुस्कुराया
यह एक थके हुए बूढ़े मल्लाह की
मुस्कान थी
जिसमें कोई पछतावा नहीं था
यदि थी तो एक सच्ची
और गहरी कृतज्ञता
बहते हुए चंचल जल के प्रति
मानो उसकी आँखें कहती हों –
'अब हो गई शाम
अच्छा भाई पानी
राम ! राम !'

I saw the Ganges

I saw the Ganges
after a long journey
When my eyes were thirsting to see anything
When I had no work to do
I saw the Ganges

after the blows of the raging hot winds
When one evening
I desperately needed
courage and freshness
I saw the Ganges, in it a Rohu fish,
in whose brimming eye
there was an infinite fluidity of living
I saw the Ganges where an old boatman
was standing on the sand
ready to go home
And I saw—
the old man was happy
even on those saddest days of the year
I was amazed to see
how long and splendid
the reflection of an old man's happiness
seemed in the water of the Ganges

The old man stirred,
lifted his net
onto his shoulder
Before going
he looked at the Ganges once more
and smiled
with the smile
of an old tired boatman
in which there was no regret
If anything
there was true and deep gratitude
towards the flowing restless water
as if his eyes were saying—
'It's evening now,
well, Water, my friend,
so long'.

Notes and References

[1] This is the first of three 'Fragments'.

[2] This is the 6th of a sequence of twenty-one poems, included in the book 'The Tiger.'

I don't accept that women's happiness is limited only to the household. Even after carefully arranging her home [a woman] doesn't feel fully satisfied, she feels incomplete. . . Living at home she fulfills her every desire, but she doesn't get the opportunity to expand intellectually. Poetry fills this gap for me.

(Shakunt Mathur in Agyeya 1996b, p.44)

Shakunt Mathur
B. 1920

Shakunt Mathur is one of the forerunners of feminism in contemporary Hindi poetry. Her life and her verses speak of the struggles of a strong-willed, gifted woman, living within the limitations imposed on her by patriarchal society. She was born in Delhi in 1920, the eldest daughter of a well-to-do family. As a young girl she participated in the Independence movement, earning the epithet 'tigress' given to her by relatives. At eighteen she broke off her engagement with a wealthy lawyer and married the promising, but not yet established, poet Girijakumar Mathur, who had first attracted her attention at a poetry reading. Most of his life he suffered ill health and Shakunt Mathur looked after him devotedly. They had six children, two of whom did not survive. What emerges from this biographical sketch is a woman of strong will who had the courage to challenge her family and marry the man of her choice, and to shoulder the burdens that came her way.

Yet Shakunt Mathur's creative persona comes across as rather diffident. As she writes in her 'Statement' (Agyeya 1996b, p.44) 'from the beginning I never thought that I was a poet and that my work could have any significance to anybody else'. Clearly poetry was very important to her–it was a path for intellectual fulfilment. But her need for self-expression seems to end with the act of writing; she has not been interested in the dissemination of her poetry. Her poems were first published thanks to the insistence of Agyeya and Ram Vilas Sharma, who, being family friends, came across them. Shakunt Mathur did not engage intellectually with the technical craft of poetry, or with literary movements, for which reason she thought that her 'poems might not possess the standard qualities of poetry' (ibid., p.45).

Most strikingly, she seems to have subjugated her creative persona to that of her husband, who established himself as one of the prominent poets of *Nayī Kavitā*. In her own words, 'whenever I write, some or other work of his comes in front of me and my poem gets embarrassed.' (ibid., p.44). Throughout Shakunt Mathur's life it has been her husband's poetry that has mattered– even now she is more worried about books of his which remain unpublished after his death, than about the publication of her own work. She started composing lyrics as a child and continued writing until her health deteriorated in the late 1980s. Despite this long poetic career she has published only three collections of poems: *Cā dnī cūnar* (Moonlight garb), *Abhī aur kuch* (Still some more) and *Lahar nahī̃ tūtegī* (The wave won't break), apart from her brilliant poetic debut in the second of Agyeya's prestigious three *Saptaks*.

For Shakunt Mathur, poetry has been a bridge into the wide world, to which she as a traditional Indian woman had no access:

> Sitting here at home I paint pictures of various cities, colourful buildings, clubs, men and women; of life moving fast, and life in dark narrow lanes and solitary villages. I peep into capitalists' warehouses and the lives of workers, coolies, stringers of charpoys, and blacksmiths.
>
> (ibid.)

However, her poems focus on her daily existence, exchanges, observations. Woman's experience and her encounters with nature are central in this poetic world.

On the jacket of her last collection Shakunt Mathur acknowledges nature– 'the constant desire to be close to nature, the journeys to beautiful places, the wandering in forests, the ceaseless attraction of the ocean'–as her principal source of inspiration. In her poetry nature can be a character in its own right (as in 'Small affairs' from the present selection) or a signifier for the emotional landscape of the lyrical 'I' (as in 'Chilka lake'). Most of Shakunt Mathur's poems illuminate woman's experience. Works like 'You should be beautiful, the house should be beautiful', 'A challenge', 'Endure' do not merely describe women's existence, but give voice to women's dissent against patriarchal oppression.

Shakunt Mathur is one of the first women poets to give expression in Hindi to the suffocation of women in the enclosures of domesticity. She asserted women's dignity and their right to creativity and managed to 'claim a bit of water', 'sky' and 'earth' not only for herself, but for all women. Yet the significance of her verses is not limited to the feminism inherent in some of them: her ability to capture nature and her insightful meditations on life give her poetry a universal appeal, which crosses the boundaries of gender.

The text of the poems is from Mathur 1960, 1968 and 1990. Her poems have been translated in Zide 1993, pp.125–6; *Yātrā* 1996, pp.98–101 and *Indian literature* 180, pp.16–17.

Shakunt   Mathur

निगाहों ने कहा

किसी की निगाहों ने कहा
आओ
भीतर इसके झरना है
बहुत से मंदिर भी देवता भी
सोचा चलूँ
दर्शन कर लूँ
किंतु घबराहट बढ़ गई
कहीं इसने बन्द कर लिए पलक
तो
मैं भी
परियों के देश में
उनके जादुई बाग़ में
सीमा की सरहद में बन्द हो जाऊँगी

Someone's eyes

Someone's eyes said,
Come
In here there's a waterfall,
many temples, gods.
I should go, I thought,
I should worship
But my alarm grew—
What if the eyes shut?
Then
I too
will be shut
in a fairy land
in a magic garden
in the last enclosure.

तुम सुंदर हो, घर सुंदर हो

जब मैं थका हुआ घर आऊँ, तुम सुंदर हो घर सुंदर हो
चाहे दिन भर बहें पसीने
कितने भी हों कपड़े सीने
बच्चा भी रोता हो गीला

आलू भी हो आधा छीला
जब मैं थका हुआ घर आऊँ, तुम सुंदर हो घर सुंदर हो
      सब तूफ़ान रुके हों घर के
      मुझको देखो आँखों भर के
      ना जूड़े में फूल सजाए
      ना तितली से वसन, न नखरे
जब मैं थका हुआ घर आऊँ, तुम सुंदर हो घर सुंदर हो
      अधलेटी हो तुम सोफ़े पर
      फॉरिन मैगज़ीन पढ़ती हो
      शीशे सा घर साफ़ पड़ा हो
      आहट पर चौंकी पड़ती हो
तुम कविता मत लिखो सलौनी, मैं काफ़ी हूँ, तुम प्रियतर हो
जब मैं थका हुआ घर आऊँ, तुम सुंदर हो घर सुंदर हो

You should be beautiful, the house should be beautiful

When I return home tired you should be beautiful, the house
      should be beautiful
      Even if all day sweat poured
      However many clothes you sewed
      Even if the child doesn't yield
      and the potato is half-unpeeled

When I return home tired you should be beautiful, the house
      should be beautiful
      All storms in the house should be stilled
      You should look at me with eyes filled
      without flowers in your hair,
      showy clothes, flirtatious air

When I return home tired you should be beautiful, the house
      should be beautiful
      Reclining on the sofa,
      you should be reading a foreign journal
      The house should shine like crystal
      My steps' sound should startle you

Don't write poetry, beauty, I am enough, you are loved
When I return home tired you should be beautiful, the house
      should be beautiful

कॉफ़ी हाऊस
ये ख़ाली वक़्त
और भरा कॉफ़ी हाऊस
एक कप कॉफ़ी

और इस क्षण का सारा का सारा दु:ख-सुख
काले
पीले
लाल, सफ़ेद
इन चेहरों में जियूँ
अनिश्चित सीढ़ियों से चढ़ी
अहसानों और पश्चात्तापों पर टँगी ज़िंदगी
आता और जाता समय
झागों-सा मिटता है
काट दी वह धार सजल जो अचानक आयी थी
छाँट दी वह कोमलांगी कुसुम-भरी शाखा
जिसने मुझे लपेटा था
पाट दिया वह भाग सारा
जहाँ ऊष्मा की गहराई थी
अब जियूँ ये क्षण
अकेला
पियूँ ये चेहरे
पेय का रंग जितना गहरा हो काला हो
अच्छा है
अतल गहराई के अनडूबे अँधेरे में
डूबूँ और घुलूँ
एक सफ़ेद चूने के
क्यूब की तरह।

Coffee House

These empty hours
Full coffee house
A cup of coffee
and all the joys and sorrows of the moment.
Black,
yellow,
red and white—
should I live
in these faces
a life
that has climbed up uncertain stairs
suspended on gratitudes and regrets?
Time, coming, going
disappears like froth.
Blocked—the stream that came unexpected
Cut—the tender, blossoming branch
that had enfolded me.

Filled up—the abyss of fire
Should I live these moments now
alone?
Drink these faces?
However deep, however black the colour of the drink
it's good
Should I sink and dissolve
like a white sugar cube[1]
in the floating darkness of the bottomless deep?

काँच

तुम्हें मालूम नहीं क्या ?
काँच एक ही झटके में
टूट जाता है
और उसकी नज़ाकत इसी में है
कि
वह टूट जाय ।

Glass

Didn't you know?
Glass breaks
at a single blow
And
its fineness is measured
by its
breaking.

चुनौती

दुनिया तेरी भी है
आकाश है
दिक् है
काल है
माना बहुत बड़ी है
माना बहुत बढ़िया है
किंतु मैंने भी तो बड़े पानी में
ढेला फेंका है
कुछ पानी घेरा है
मैं बाँहें फैलाये खड़ी हूँ
कुछ आकाश घेरा है
मैं पृथ्वी पर लेटी हूँ
मैंने कुछ पृथ्वी घेरी है

मैंने भावना से जो कुछ जोड़ा है
मैं कह सकती हूँ
इतना यह सब मेरा है।

A challenge

   You too have a world–
  Sky
   Horizon
  Time
   True–it's enormous
   True–it's excellent!
But I too have cast
a clod into the deep
and claimed a bit of water.
I've stood with arms spread
and claimed a bit of sky.
I've lain on the earth
and claimed a bit of earth
Whatever I've gathered with passion
That much I can say:
It all is mine.

सहना

सहना,
कभी किसी से, कुछ न कहना
चार दीवारी की एक ईंट सी
उसी में लगी रहना

कबूतर रंगों वाला आएगा ज़रूर
उड़ जाएगा तुझे वहाँ न देख
तू कटोरी भर पानी भी अब
कभी भी न रखना

समो भीतर ही भीतर सब कुछ अपना
भूल कर भी किसी को
आकर्षित न करना
उस पत्थर की तरह
जिसको लांघ ऊपर से झरना निकल जाय
ऐसे रहना।

तू चुप रह
चुप्पी हवा की
चुप्पी गगन की
समुद्र की

पृथ्वी की
तेरे लिए
तू चुप ही रहना
कभी किसी से कुछ न कहना

आन्तरिक पत्तों की सूखी खनखन
आन्तरिक पुष्पों की एक एक
पंखुरी झरन
बुझा अंगार
बुझा समुद्ध का अंतर
कोई न देखे
सहना !
अब तू चुप ही रहना
कभी किसी से कुछ न कहना

Endure

Endure,
never say anything to anybody

Like a brick in an enclosing wall
remain fixed

A colourful pigeon will surely come
and fly away without seeing you
Don't ever keep
even a bowl of water
Settle everything inside you,
don't attract anybody
even by mistake
Live like a stone
above which a waterfall may flow

Be silent
The silence of the air
the sky
the ocean
the earth
is for you
Be silent
Never say anything to anybody

No one should notice
No one should notice
the withered rustle of the inner leaves,
the falling off

of every petal
of the inner flowers,
the extinguished spark,
the heart of the subdued ocean
Endure!
Be silent
Never say anything to anybody.

छोटी छोटी बातें
नन्हीं चिड़िया
पेड़ के ऊपर से उड़ गई
पेड़ ने दृष्टि भर घूरा
नीला आकाश
और नीचे झुक आया
डरी हुई जड़ों ने
धरती को और कस
लिया।

Small affairs

A little bird
on a tree
flew away.
The tree stared for a moment
at the blue sky
and bent down.
Frightened, its roots
drew the earth
tighter.

चिलका झील
ये किसी की नींद है
जो फैली है
उस लोक की तरह जिसे कोई
छू नहीं गया है
इसके भीतर जो सपना डूबा था
वह जाग रहा है
कुछ न कह सकने की स्थिति में –
कोई बड़ी नाव यहाँ डूबी थी
इसके गर्भ में
इसीलिए ये झील

इतनी शान्त
इसकी गहरी काली, बड़ी-बड़ी आँखें इतनी शान्त
इसकी उठती हुई इधर-उधर की पहाड़ियाँ
इसके उत्तर में चलती नावें इतनी शान्त –

सुना था
ये समुद्र ही का एक भाव है
किन्तु समुद्र कितना उन्मादी
उसका भीषण गर्जन
जलदी-जलदी उठती-गिरती
अजदही सरकती लहरें –
और ये झील–
जिसके बीचोबीच एक अतिथि गृह
लोक आते हैं, ठहरते हैं
चले जाते हैं
स्तब्ध हिरनों के झुण्ड
खड़े देखते रह जाते हैं–
आज कोई नहीं यहाँ
बाहर-भीतर सन्नाटा
रात गहरी है
मैं और तुम
तुम और मैं
मैं भी नहीं
हम दोनों ही नहीं
सिर्फ़ इस झील की गहराई
जिसमें कोई नाव डूबी थी –

Chilka lake

This—someone's sleep
stretched
like the world
untouched by anyone
The dream that drowned in it
is waking
speechless
A large boat sunk here—
in its womb
And so this lake
Its huge deep black eyes—so peaceful
Its hillocks rising here and there
The boats following them—so peaceful
I've heard this to be

a pose of the ocean
But the ocean is so frenzied
Its fearsome roar
Its python-waves
swiftly rising and falling
And this lake–
In its midst a shelter
People come and stay,
leave
Flocks of startled deer
watch on.

Nobody's here today
Quiet in and out
The night is deep
I and you
You and I
Not even me
Not even us
Only the deep of this lake
in which a boat once sunk.

Notes and References

[1] *Cūnā* literally means 'lime'; the translation 'sugar cube' seems better to me and has been approved by the author.

*In front of the reader rises a poetic personality in which there isn't the black
colouring of frustration and despair, despite all the pain and suffering; in which
there is the power to grasp nature's most delicate sensations; there is freshness,
joy and the essence of dreams.*

(Prabha 1996b, introductory page 7)

Kanta
1934–1986

These few lines from Muktibodh's review of Kanta's first collection *Jo kuch bhī
dekhtī hū̃* (Whatever I see) summarise her poetic sensibility: pain is the
prevailing colour in her emotional palette, yet it is not the black of despair;
nature is the main presence in her work, both as a backdrop and as a character
in its own right. While nature is all-pervading in Kanta's poetry, the social
world is absent. Her poems paint the emotional landscapes of her lyrical heroine
with single-minded dedication. In this way they are reminiscent of the
monochromatic subject matter of Mahadevi Verma's[1] poetry, which draws the
image of the woman, consumed by the fire of love in separation, the *virahinī*,
awaiting the return of her beloved with humble self-surrender. However,
whereas Mahadevi Verma's poetic sensibility owes much to earlier
philosophical and devotional traditions, Kanta's is decisively modern. And
yet the omnipresence of sorrow and the pre-eminence of love connect the two
poets, even if in Kanta the Buddhist and *bhakti* links are not so readily traceable.

In poem after poem Kanta paints different shades of pain, loneliness, absence
and unfulfilled desire. The mindscape of the lyrical heroine is imposed on the
landscape: darkness, smoke, clouds, sky, fire, sea and sand are common signifiers
of emotion in Kanta's work. Death is a constant, yet most poems avoid the
trap of self-pity and self-indulgence. Instead works like 'Sorrow–a smell' from
the present selection echo with self-mockery and reveal Kanta's sense of the
absurd, her irony.

Kanta's productivity within such restrictive co-ordinates is unique–unlike
Mahadevi Verma (who wrote only prose in the last forty-five years of her life),
Kanta continued writing poetry for almost thirty years until her tragic death

of cancer in 1986. Whereas her early lyrics are conceived as individual pieces
and usually have titles, her later poems, longer and untitled, merge in a more
fluid way to create an alternative dream-like world. Both her early and late
works are beautifully crafted and free of the obscurity characteristic of some of
Nayī Kavitā.

Perhaps Kanta managed to sustain her writing because it sustained her. Her
later poems in particular suggest the importance of self-expression to her.
However, it seems that, like Shakunt Mathur, Kanta was uninterested in the
dissemination of her work, demonstrated by the fact that most of her poetry
remained unpublished in her lifetime. Her sister Prabha published two
collections of her poetry, *Kāntā-smṛti: kāvyakār* 1 and 2 (in memory of Kanta:
The form of poetry 1 and 2), which included poems written between 1961 and
1985, and a collection of her songs *Kāntā-gītsmṛti* (Kanta's lyrics) posthumously.
Kanta's reluctance to impose herself is demonstrated also by her refusal to
write introductory notes to her poetry, because, as the jacket of her second
collection of poems *Samayātī* (Time past) asserts, a poet's statements are 'an
intervention between the poetry and its reader'.

Having sketched a few basic characteristics of Kanta's poetry, let us trace
some of the formative influences upon her. She was born in Hyderabad in a
well-to-do family and grew up in an atmosphere saturated with literature, arts
and politics. Her older brother Badrivishal Pitti was a long-serving editor of
Kalpanā, one of the most respected literary journals of the time. Kanta did a BA
in Arts and got married into a traditional family. She rebelled against the
limitations imposed on her by the expectation that she would be a traditional
daughter-in-law, and the marriage broke up. Kanta devoted the rest of her life
to literature: she helped edit *Kalpanā* and *Kṛti*, wrote literary criticism, and
made a very successful translation of Anna Akhmatova's poetry from English
into Hindi which was published as a special issue of the magazine *Tanāv* in
1984.[2]

Reading this personal history and 'Walls upon walls' from the present
selection, one might be tempted to lable Kanta a feminist poet, as an MPhil
thesis written at the University of Hyderabad (G. Singh, 2000) does. However,
her poetry reveals a more complex picture which again is reminiscent of
Mahadevi Verma. Like Mahadevi, Kanta rebelled against the enclosure of a
traditional marriage and chose to shape her own path. And yet Kanta's lyrics,
like Mahadevi's, are not feminist (at least in the narrow sense of this word):
they are steeped in loneliness, in yearning for love and in the grief of unfulfilled
desire to be a mother. It is to Kanta's credit that the painful price she paid for
her freedom did not push her into resentment, bitterness or self-pity, that she
found the inner strength to 'gather [her] darkness inside' and not destroy 'the
sunlight'. Kanta's poetic voice is not loud; self-promotion and
self-congratulation are not in its tonality. It has not been heard by literary

critics or translators. Yet it is clear, pure and powerful if one has ears for its dreamy, sad beauty.

The text of the poems is taken from Kanta 1960 and 1964, Prabha 1996a and b, and *Kalpanā*, May 1964. I have not been able to find any previous translations of Kanta's poetry. The only existent study of Kanta's work is G. Singh 2000.

Notes and References

1 Mahadevi Verma (1907–1987) is one of the famous four poets of *Chāyāvād*. The other three are Nirala, Sumitranandan Pant and Jayshankar Prasad.
2 The impact that Kanta's translation had on the Hindi literary world can be surmised from the fact that Shamsher Bahadur Singh dedicated a poem to it– *Ākhmātovākī kavitāō ke kāntākṛt anuvād paṛhne ke bād*', 'After reading Kanta's translation of Akhmatova's poetry (Singh 1988, p.64).

Kanta

धुआँ

आज जब
अँधेरे के वक्ष पर माथा टेक रो चुकी हूँ,
सहज हूँ,
समझ पा रही हूँ,
कि वे
शब्द—केवल शब्द—थे,
जो मैंने अब तक उचारे।
इसीलिए जब भी कुछ उनसे जन्मा
तो वह मात्र धुआँ रहा : दुराग्रही—
        फैल कर
अग्नि की मरण की कथा
सबको सुनाता रहा !

Smoke

Today
calm
after a cry with head rested on the bosom of darkness
I can understand
that those
words uttered by me
were nothing more than words.
So whatever was born of them
remained mere smoke: stubborn—
        it spread
telling everybody again and again
the tale of fire's death!

सुख

मैंने वह सब लिया,
जो चाहे अनचाहे मिला :
सूरजमुखी-सी हँसी
खूब तेज़ हवा में उखड़ते
पुराने पीपल के पत्तों का ऋन्दन
स्निग्ध धूप-सी झलमलाती अकारण
आतुर खुशियाँ

दबे पाँव पास आते अंधकार-सा
विवश परिताप भी।

और हर बार सुखी हुई।
किन्तु सुख यह।
गूँगे के स्वाद-सा अनभिव्यक्त,
इकतरफ़ा-चाहना-सा
अनलौटाया रहा, रहा–
मुझ में रहा।

Happiness

I took it all,
wanted or not:
sunflower-like smile,
the lament of the old pipal tree's leaves
scattered in the wild wind,
the causeless impatient joys
sparkling like shiny sunlight,
the helpless anguish
approaching stealthily like darkness.

And every time I was happy.
But that happiness
unexpressed like a taste on a mute's tongue,
like a one-sided desire
remained unreturned, remained
inside me.

डूब गये हैं संकेत

डूब गये हैं संकेत
सुख के, दुख के, प्रेम के !

है, गहरा है मौन यह!
इसमें डूब गया है अंधकार,
वाचाल अंधकार

Traces

Sunk–the traces
of joy, sorrow, love!

Deep–this silence!
In which darkness drowned,
garrulous darkness.

दीवारों पर दीवारें

दीवारें तो बहुत थीं।
फिर भी जीवित था मुझमें
एक हरा पौधा !
– रोज़ छूती थी उसे
छनती हुई किरन
पहले से और ज्यादा जिलाने:
रोज़ आते थे पंछी
उस पर
अपनी ख़ुश फरफराहटें बिखेरने !

पर अब तो केवल
छत से सटी हुई
दीवारों पर दीवारें !
दरवाज़ों–खिड़कियों पर दीवारें !!

Walls upon walls

As for walls there were many.
Still a green sapling
was alive in me.
–Every day a sun ray filtered through
and touched it
to give it more life.
Every day birds came
to scatter on it
the happy flutter of their wings!

But now
all the way up to the ceiling
only walls upon walls!
Over doors and windows
walls!

रोड–लैम्प का मंदा–मंदा आलोक,
और पानी, झिलमिलाता पानी,
और डूबा–डूबा सा आकाश,
और तुम, और मैं :
बेतरतीब हरियाली पर।
फिर भी जैसे
न तुम, न मैं, न कोई और ही।
केवल पानी।
पानी :

एक क्षण झिलमिलाता
एक क्षण
अँधेरे से ढँका हुआ ।

The faint light of the street lamps
and water, shimmering water,
and sunken skies,
and you, and me:
on the disorderly green.
Still, it's as if
there is no you, no me, nobody else.
Only water.
Water:
now shimmering
now
covered in dark!

धूप चमक रही थी
इस पेड और उस पेड़ :
लपक कर तोड़ लूँ :
कुछ ऐसा मन हुआ !
पर बच्चे वहाँ खेल रहे थे,
धूप बटोर रहे थे !
हँसी को
हवाओं में उछाल रहे थे!
–मैं बिना आवाज़ धीरे–से
          बढ़ गयी
अपने–आप में अपना अँधकार समेटे ।

The sunlight was shining
on this tree and that tree.
I felt like
catching it, breaking it!
But children were playing there,
gathering up the sunlight!
Tossing their laughter
in the wind!
–I moved on

        silently, slowly
Gathering my darkness inside me.

    ◇

हल्की-हल्की लालिमा
      आकाश पर
और फेन-से बादल –
अस्त
होती जा रही हूँ मैं
वह रही है सिर्फ़
हवा के संग
एर गूँज, एक पुकार।

    ◇

Slight blush
    on the sky
and foam-like clouds—
I am
sinking
Only an echo, a call
floating
with the wind.

    ◇

आकाश और आकाश के बीच
मैं
विभाजन-रेख-सी :
न इधर, इस पार,
न उधर, उस पार।
– यही मेरी नियति !
यही मेरा महत्व !! ।
कोई आए, मुझे तोड़ ले।
दे दे
इस पार की रोशनी, या,
उस पार का अंधकार :
कोई एक निश्चिति !

    ◇

Between sky and sky
I
a division line:
neither here, on this side

nor there, on that.
–This is my fate!
My significance!

Come, break me.
Give me
the light of this side, or
the darkness of that:
some resolution!

◇

अंधेरे-सी छा गयी हूँ
आकाश पर :
बहुत ही उदास-सी बात कहो एक ।
बरस जाएँ
मेरी परतों के नीचे जमे बादल ।

◇

I am spread like darkness
on the sky:
Tell me something very sad.
So that the clouds gathered underneath my folds
may rain.

◊

पृथ्वी को पैरों तले रौंदता
दौड़ा जा रहा है समय ।
मैं-उसकी पीठ पर किलबिलाता
        जीवन का एक टुकड़ा –
फिसल कर गिर रही हूँ ।

◇

Time, running,
tramples the earth under its feet.
I–a piece of life
    wriggling on its back–
am sliding off.

◇

बच्चे की बाँहों-सा मचला
        मन   .
            सहम गया ।
बरौनियों पर अटकी

तरल हँसी के बदले
एक सर्द हँसी ।

◇

Unruly like a child's arms
    the mind
        was scared–
Lingering on the eyelashes
    instead of a tremulous smile
cold laughter.

◇

प्रतीक्षा
सपनों में बीत गयी रात–कभी,
अक्सर
गरमी का दिन लम्बा ।

◇

Waiting
sometimes–a night passed in dreaming.
Often
a long hot day.

◇

गो, यह सच,
मुट्ठियाँ कसे आता है
किंतु बडा सच तो यही
कि हथेलियाँ फैला कर
हवा में फैल जाता है
    जीवन ।
क्यों बाँधूँ सपने?
क्यों समेटूँ आँखों में
पीड़ा?
क्यों कहीं भी लुटा लूँ मन ?
सुख तो, बस,
    एकांत एकांत –गायन !

◇

Though it is true
that it arrives with tight fists
the Truth is

that opening its palms,
    life
expands in the air.
Why tie my dreams?
Why gather sorrow
in my eyes?
Why bring down my mind anywhere?
Happiness?
    Just solitude–singing!

◇

. . . दुख तो एक गंध।
कहीं से आती नहीं, इसीलिए
कहीं जाती नहीं
बस, फैलती है
      अपनी गंधहीनता में–निःशंक।
अंधेरे में होती उजागर
और धूप भी ढांक पाती नहीं उसे
वह
   केवल आकाश
      और आकाश है।
जिंदगी के अकेले और भीड़ भरे
क्षणों में
लगता, गंध यह
एक जगह सिमट आयी
   या, छितर गयी।
निर्बंध, फिर भी,
फिर भी,
   सहज
बीती यादों की तरह
   यहीं, यहीं, बस–यहीं।
और. . .
इसी ऐसे दुख पर रोने के लिए
आदमी
   जागता है रात
      कितनी हंसी की है बात।

◇

. . . Sorrow–a smell.
It comes from nowhere, so
it goes nowhere,
  just spreads
    fearless in its smell-lessness

It is radiant in darkness
Sunlight can't conceal it either
It is
    only air
        air.
In the lonely and crowded
moments of life
it seems that this smell
gathered in one place,
    or diffused.
Unbound, yet
    natural,
like past memories
    just here, just–here.
And. . .
How ludicrous it is
that man
    stays up all night
        to cry for such sorrow.

◇

पहाड़ कर लेना है पार
    सीढ़ी चढ़ जाना
कुहरे में बारिश में
अपनी छाया गढ़ पाना ।
    घबराता नहीं अब
    अंधेरे का बढ़ आना –

◇

Cross the mountain
    climb the stairs

Learn to cast your shadow
in fog and in rain.

    Now you won't be scared
    as darkness approaches–

Amrita Bharati is probably the most alone signature on the slate of contemporary Hindi poetry. Alone and unique.

(Nirmal Verma)

Amrita Bharati
B.1939

This is how the prominent Hindi fiction writer Nirmal Verma starts his appreciation of Amrita Bharati's poetry, published on the jacket of her last collection 'Man ruk gayā vahā̃' (The mind stopped there). He is right–her life story and her poetry single her out, sentence her to both loneliness and solitude. It is incredibly difficult to write about her, to crystallise a lifelong spiritual quest into down-to-earth biographical details, more so because the conservative society of her youth chose to sentence her to oblivion for her naive love for a married man–and, perhaps more importantly, because of her humility, which has made her shy away from the public eye. Nothing has been written about Amrita Bharati: there are no studies of her poetry, no bibliographical material; her name is not currency in Hindi poetic circles. Despite her six collections of poems, a volume of prose and numerous translations from English, she has remained unrecognized.

When I met Amrita Bharati her first words about herself were that she was living on two different levels: that of worldly existence and that of a spiritual quest. Her struggle with the former and her deep attachment to the latter permeate her poetry. In her early work the existential angst prevails. Poems like 'An ongoing role' in the selection here speak of intense suffering, of an apocalyptic tragedy in which the female protagonist becomes 'Agony'. 'From the very first day' and 'Far into the stillness' add anger to her emotional palette: it is the collective anger of womanhood, suppressed for centuries by patriarchy. 'The second question' is a witness to Amrita Bharati's social conscience–her poetry gives voice not only to women's suffering, but also to that of the poor, 'the eternal pain of countless men'. It is exactly the agony, the pain and the anger which have brought about the spiritual quest. The last collection, represented by 'The mind stopped', 'But' and 'In the stillness of the word', shows the destination–a refuge of serenity where 'the mind stops' and the anguished protagonist finds her self and Him. For Amrita Bharati poetry is not just a witness, but her guide, which brings her closer to herself and God.

It is a commonplace that poetry maps the outer and inner wanderings of the poet's life. But it is the sheer distance covered in Amrita Bharati's emotional journey which is fascinating. There are many poets, and less gifted humans, who travel through torment. But not many emerge into a land of serenity and love, rather than of disenchantment and cynicism. Moreover, the change in the emotional landscape of the protagonist is accompanied by a growing simplicity in poetic form. Her early long poems, marked by elaborate images and Sanskrit loanwords, give way to the short, beautifully simple poems in *Man ruk gayā vahā̃*.

Having sketched Amrita Bharati's inner trajectory let us return to the outer level and try to outline the external events which influenced her sensibility. She was born in Najibabad (UP) in an Arya Samaj family. Her father was a social reformer who had dedicated his life to helping people in need. Her mother, a saintly woman, brought up eight children and assisted her husband in his work. It seems neither of them had much time to build up the confidence of the young, over-sensitive Amrita. She did an MA and PhD in Sanskrit at Benares Hindu University. Interested in Sanskrit poetics, she wrote her thesis on the 8th-century Sanskrit playwright and poet Bhavabhuti. Her intimacy with words, her awareness of their etymology, evolution and hidden meanings, which is so conspicuous in her work, must have been enhanced by her studies. She started writing poetry as a student in Benares. After graduation she taught Sanskrit in Lucknow, Bombay and Delhi for several years. In the 1970s she edited the literary magazine *Paśyantī*.

Amrita's spiritual journey began early in her childhood. When she was about eight years old she read about the penance of the Vishnu devotee Prahlad and this set her on a spiritual quest she has followed throughout her life. In the late 1970s this search took her to Sri Aurobindo's ashram in Delhi. She has been living in his ashram in Pondicherry for several years.

However, this striving for the Truth has not cut her off from the truth of her reality. Her book of prose demonstrates the broad spectrum of her concerns: from the situation in India, to Marxism, from Che Guevara to George Orwell and Jawaharlal Nehru. Her writing presents the exotic combination of spiritual leaning and progressive/leftist commitment. Not only her subject matter, but also the genres she employs are varied: essays, editorials, diary and letters. She has written literary criticism on and translated the works of Hölderlin, Kathleen Raine, Boris Pasternak and George Seferis. Indian literature too has moved her to write literary appreciation: her essays on 'the father of Hindi prose' Premchand, the Sanskrit poet and playwright Kalidas, and Muktibodh are personal and insightful at the same time. She has also translated Sri Aurobindo's sonnets and some of his other poems.

'Mysticism' or even 'spiritual surrealism' are labels used to describe Amrita Bharati's poetry in the few pieces of literary appreciation of her work published on the jackets of her books. Though catchy, they do not capture the intense quality of Amrita Bharati's poetry, her suffering and her serenity, her courage to seek beauty and love even when surrounded by small-mindedness and poverty. It is this visionary power of turning the deepest dark into gentle light which singles her out, makes her 'the most alone signature on the slate of contemporary Hindi poetry.'

The texts of the poems are from Bharati 1978, 1992 and 2000. A few of her poems are translated in Zide 1993, p.23; Yātrā 1996, pp.93–7 and *Indian literature* 180, pp.35–7.

Amrita   Bharati

एक चल रही भूमिका

जूडिथ ने एक नाटक देखा था
उसमें मैं 'यातना' की भूमिका कर रही थी।

दुनिया मंच की तरह फैल गयी थी
और वक़्त पर्दे की तरह उठा था
मैंने अपने किसी भी टुकड़े को
बाहर छोड़े बग़ैर   अन्दर
प्रवेश किया था।

(नाटक इससे पहले भी खेला गया था –
दुनिया मंच की तरह फैली थी
वक़्त पर्दे की तरह उठा था
लेकिन मैं यह नहीं कह सकती
कि मेरी यह कौन सी बारी थी
पहली दूसरी या सौवीं।)
जूडिथ ने एक नाटक देखा था
उसने देखा था
कि मैं भूमिका को
भूमिका की तरह नहीं कर रही हूँ
और उसमें से बाहर निकलने की कोशिश कर रही हूँ

मतलब
मैं दर्शकों में आ जाना चाहती हूँ
और उन्हें भी पार कर
प्रेक्षागृह का दरवाज़ा खोल
बाहर
सड़क पर
और कोढ़ी के हाथ को
प्रेमि के हाथ की तरह छूना चाहती हूँ
पर बात सिर्फ़ इतनी ही नहीं थी
और सूत्रधार चिन्तित था।
जूडिथ ने एक नाटक देखा था
और डर कर
तब उसने आँखें बन्द कर ली थीं
जब देखा था
कि मैं भूमिका से सच्चे पात्र में उत्तर आयी हूँ
और मेरे साथ

वह सारी रंग सज्जा –मसलन
रेशमी कांटों के मुकुट क्रुस और कीलें
ज़हर के प्यालों का पानी
ख़ून की जगह छिड़का हुआ रंग
और वह अदालत
और वे सब लोग भी
– जज जूरी नगरजन और मुख़बिर
अपनी अपनी भूमिका में –नाटक से
बाहर निकल आये हैं ।

जूडिथ ने एक नाटक देखा था
उसके मुंह से चीख़ निकल गयी थी
जब उसने देखा था
कि अब कोई नेपथ्य भी नहीं रहा
ईश्वर ने अपने को
आदमी के क़ानून के हवाले कर दिया है
और मैं
सड़क के बीचो बीच
एक पत्थर पर सिर रखकर रो रही हूँ ।
जूडिथ ने एक नाटक देखा था
जिसमें मैं 'यातना' की भूमिका कर रही थी
जूडिथ बेहोश हो गयी थी यह देखकर
कि पाप के बोझ के नीचे झुका ईश्वर
वचनमुक्त हो चुका है
और दुनिया का नक़्शा
गोल पत्थर के साथ   धीरे धीरे
मेरे कन्धों की तरफ़ सरक रहा है ।
जूडिथ ने एक नाटक देखा था
और   वह नहीं देख सकी थी
कि मंच का दरवाज़ा मेरे हाथ नहीं आ रहा
और मेरे चारों तरफ़
पर्दे गिर चुके हैं ।

An ongoing role

Judith saw a play
in which I was acting 'Agony'.
The world was stretched like a stage
Time lifted like a curtain
I   entered
not leaving any
part of me out
[The play had been performed before–

The world stretched like a stage
Time lifted like a curtain–
But I can't tell
how many times I've played–
one, two, hundreds.]
Judith saw a play
Saw
that I wasn't acting my role
like a role,
but trying to come out of it

I mean
I wanted to go into the audience
and beyond
To open the theatre door
and go out
into the street
I wanted to touch a leper's hand
like a lover's
But it wasn't just that
and the stage-manager was worried.

Judith saw a play
Scared
she closed her eyes
when she saw
that I had become the real character
And with me
all the props–
the crown of silken thorns, the cross and the nails,
the water in the chalice of poison,
the dye, sprinkled instead of blood,
and the court,
and all the people
–the judge, the jury, the townsfolk and the spies
Each in their role–coming out
of the play

Judith saw a play
She screamed
when she saw
that there was no backstage anymore
God
had entrusted himself to the law of man

And I
was crying in the middle of the street
My head placed on a stone

Judith saw a play
in which I was acting 'Agony'
She fainted when she saw
God, bent under the burden of sin,
speechless
And the map of the world
on a round stone slowly
sliding onto my shoulders.

Judith saw a play
But she didn't see
that my hand couldn't find the stage door
And all around me
the curtain had fallen.

दूसरा सवाल

मन्दिर के बाहर
वे किसकी आँखें थीं–
शरीर से तो वह पूरा नहीं था
जगह–जगह झरा हुआ
खाया हुआ
गला हुआ –
पर आँखें
उनमें ग्लानि और यन्त्रणा का इतिहास
पुराना हो चुका था,
जो नया था
वह था उसके अन्दर का झाँकता कोई एक प्रकाशित कोना
और रोकता हुआ–सा
एक सवाल –
मैंने उस प्रकाशित कोने को तो स्वीकार किया
पर सवाल से बचकर आगे जाने की कोशिश की
लेकिन वह तो आड़ा हो गया वह सवाल
ठीक एक खूँटी की तरह
मानो मेरे सारे कपड़े उतार लेगा –
मैंने पीछे हटकर अपनी असमर्थता जाहिर की
पर वह चीख उठा
'और कब तक?'
मैं रुक गयी।
मैंने सवाल को बटोरा
और उसके दो टुकड़े कर दिये

एक में वह था
वह एक अकेला आदमी
और नियत अवधि से जुड़ी उसकी यन्त्रणा
उसे मैंनं अपने अन्दर रखा
क्योंकि मैं स्वयं इस समय एक अवधि के अन्दर थी
और यही उसका उत्तर था।

पर दूसरा
आदमी की असंख्यता से जुड़ा था- निरवधि
समष्टिगत यन्त्रणा से।
मैं उसे वहीं
धरती की प्रतिक्षा की तरह खुलि
निश्चल हथेली पर छोड़
मन्दिर की सीढ़ियाँ चढ़ गयी।

The second question

Whose eyes were those
outside the temple?
His body–incomplete
All shrunk
Eaten away
Emaciated–
And the eyes
Their history of hate and pain
was already ancient
But there was something new–
A lit corner inside him, peeping out,
and a suppressed
question–
I accepted the lit corner
but tried to escape the question, to move on
It obstructed me–that question
Just like a peg
greedy for my clothes–

Stepping back I showed my helplessness
But he suddenly screamed
'How much longer?'
I stood still
I gathered the question
And split it into two
In one half was he
That man alone
and his life-sentence–

Locked in the same time-frame
I placed him inside me
This was his answer

But the other half–
That of the eternal pain
of countless men
I left it there
on the motionless palm
opened like earth's waiting
And climbed up the temple stairs

वही   एक घटना

वह औरत का दिल था
जो बोल रहा था
बोले ही जा रहा था
युगों से ।
वह औरत का दिल था
जो चुप था

चुप चला आ रहा था
सदियों से

और इनके बीच एक पहाड़ था
एक आदमी या
एक चूहा
जो कुतर रहा था
मित्र क्षणों में भी
चीतकार करती आवाज़ को
सुन्न हुई जुबान को
पहले ही दिन से ।

From the very first day

It was a woman's heart
which was talking
Had been talking
for ages
It was a woman's heart
which was silent
Had been silent
for centuries

Between them–a mountain
A man or
A rat

which was gnawing
even in moments of intimacy
at the screaming voice
at the still tongue
from the very first day

सन्नाटे में दूर तक

उन्होंने मुझे
ढेले की तरह फेंका था
वे नहीं जानते थे
मैं एक आत्मवस्तु हूँ
वे यह भी नहीं जानते थे
कि मैं एक जीवित वस्तु हूँ

वे मुझे
ढेले की तरह फेंकते रहे
अपने रास्ते से अलग
उस 'परित्यक्त पथ' पर, जो
संयोग से मेरा था।
और इस तरह मैं
अपने रास्ते की
दूरी तय करती रही।
हर बार झर जाता कोई कण
आसक्ति का कोई भाव, सुख की कोई संलग्नता
धरती से जुड़ी कोई आशा
आदमी में फैला कोई स्वप्न
हर बार झर जाता
मेरे अस्तित्व का कोई कण
और अब मेरी बारी थी
पीछे छूट चुका था विश्व–
रेतीले अन्धड़ से भरे मरुस्थल की तरह
तूफ़ानी महासमुद्र और
सूने नगर की तरह–
पीछे छूट चुका था
हर पग नीची सीढ़ियाँ उतरता आदमी
और अब यह मेरी बारी थी।
धरती के आख़िरी टुकड़े पर खड़े हो मैंने
अपने को
पूर्ण वस्तु की तरह समेटा था।
और प्रक्षेपित किया था।
सन्नाटे में
यह मेरी नीरवता थी–
व्यास और विस्तृत।

अब विश्व या तो एक सपना था
या दूर प्रतिभासित होता
एक जल-पुष्प
इस पारावार में
सन्नाटे में दूर तक
मेरी ही आहट थी ।

Far into the stillness

He threw
me like a clod of earth
He didn't know
I had a soul
Nor did he know
I was alive

Again and again
he threw me like a clod of earth
away from his road
onto the deserted path
chance had made mine.
And so
I journeyed on
along my way
Each time a bit of me broke off–
attractions, attachment to happiness,
earthly hopes,
dreams scattered in man
Each time a bit of my existence
broke off

And now it was my turn

The world was already left behind–
like a desert full of dust-storm,
a turbulent ocean,
a desolate city–
Man, each of his steps descending,
was already behind

And now it was my turn

Standing on the last piece of earth,
I gathered all of me
and hurled myself
into the stillness
This was my silence–
All-pervading

Now the world was a dream
or an image
of a flower
far in the ocean
Far into the stillness
the sound of my footsteps

मन रुक गया वहाँ
मन
रुक गया वहाँ
जहाँ वह था
नित्य और निरन्तर
गतिशील
लय की अनन्तता में

मन
रुक गया वहाँ
उसके अन्दर
जहाँ घर था।

The mind stopped
The mind
stopped
where He was
Eternal, constant,
moving
in the infinitude of rhythm
The mind
stopped
inside Him
Where home was.

लेकिन
उसे
मेरे पास होना चाहिए था
यह नियत था
कि वह मेरे पास हो।
उसने कहा,
'मैं हूँ' . . .
और शेष शब्द
उसकी विनम्र चुप्पी में खो गये–
उनमें

एक 'लेकिन' था–
लेकिन ...और मैं समझ गयी थी–
मैं ही कहाँ थी
अपने पास
कि वह मेरे पास हो ।

But

He
should have been near me
It was ordained
that He should be near me
He said,
'I am . . .'
The remaining words
lost in His gentle silence–

Among them
a 'but'–

But, . . . I understood–
How could he be near me
when I wasn't
near myself?

शब्द की शान्ति में

दोनों चीज़ें
कितनी मिली-जुली हैं
उसकी धरती
मेरा आकाश ।
मैं चाहती थी
उसका अनुसरण
जहाँ भी वह हो ।

पर पथ
कितने अलग थे
एक पर वह था
दूसरे पर मैं
और बीच में एक रेखा थी
उसकी भी
मेरी भी ।

हम
कितने एक थे
अपनी आत्मा में
पर
वह चल रहा था

धरती के नीचे शिखरों पर–
और मैं
आकाश की
ऊँची खाइयों में ।

शायद
ये दोनों पथ मुड़ जायें
एक दिन
मेरी कविता में
और हम साथ–साथ चल सकें
शब्द की शान्ति में ।

In the stillness of the word

These two
are so alike–
His earth
and my sky

I wanted
to follow Him
wherever He was

But our paths
were so different
He was on one
I on the other
A line in the middle–
His
and mine

How undivided
we were
in our soul
But
He was walking
on the low summits of the earth–
and I
in the high chasms of the sky
Maybe
these two paths will turn
one day
in my poetry
and we'll walk together
in the stillness of the word

Writing is for me the 'space' where I can be; saving this space is the condition for my existence.

(Milan 1995, p.38)

Jyotsna Milan
B.1941

With Jyotsna Milan's poetry we enter a world where creative writing is not a favourite pastime, not merely an inner urge, but the condition for the poet's existence. From a very early age writing has given Jyotsna Milan the courage to enjoy her life despite the domestic drudgery that is obligatory for a girl of her generation. In her own words:

> Mother taught me all the household chores from cooking to sewing and knitting . . . and I still do them. Whatever I may be writing–poems, stories, novels–afterwards I can do the work I don't like with some interest, as long as I am writing something. In fact I write very little, but even so I don't know what I would have done without writing . . . (ibid.)

Jyotsna's childhood was ruled by two forces: a traditional mother who wanted her daughter to learn all the skills of a successful housewife, and, rather unusually for that generation, a progressive father who, being a writer himself, encouraged her to write. Her father was extremely influential in the creation of her identity as a poet: he was her first reader and helped her build an unshakable belief in the value of poetry. Unlike many female poets of her generation and before, Jyotsna grew up with a confidence in her creative abilities, enhanced also by her education: her MA in Gujarati literature was followed by one in English literature. Exposed to both Hindi and Gujarati as a child she has been creative in both languages.

Jyotsna Milan accepted the traditional life choices for a woman as a wife and a mother, and married a fellow-poet, Ramesh Chandra Shah. But she has also remained loyal to 'her first love–the written word' (ibid., p.37) and published two collections of short stories, two novels and two volumes of poetry. She has also written about and translated Gujarati poetry; for the last sixteen years she has been editing the women's journal *Anasūyā*, published by the Self-Employed Women Association (SEWA). The uneasy symbiosis between Jyotsna Milan's inheritance from her mother and that from her father is reflected in all her writing. She is painfully aware of the patriarchal restrictions and much of her poetry speaks with an eloquent feminist voice. 'Woman', included in this selection, is one of the most forceful feminist statements in Hindi poetry. Though Jyotsna Milan does not call herself a feminist poet and does not set out to be one, woman's experience is unmistakably the prism of her creativity. All her poems in this selection reflect different aspects of woman's life: the sacrifice of motherhood ('Night'); the shackles imposed on women ('Feet'); the cruel erasure of women's personal history ('Behind'); woman's loneliness ('She') and the emptiness of her existence ('Words'). Woman's search for a true home is a recurring motif in Jyotsna Milan's writing, and so is an exposure of the real nature of what is perceived to be woman's home–nothing but an enclosure where women are locked in domestic drudgery. 'Some other place' and 'Search' exemplify this motif; its centrality in Jyotsna Milan's writing is reflected by the fact that the name of one of her collections of poems is *Ghar nahī̃* (Not a home). It is hardly surprising then that many of Jyotsna Milan's poems are imbued with a yearning for freedom ('Together in the mirror', 'Sky').

Nature is the doorway to freedom in her poetry. This reflects her personal experience:

> I had to help my mother in the kitchen a lot of the time, but my mind used to wander off. I would not hear what my mother said and was often scolded for this. A parallel world would be born inside me, around me, like magic . . . Whatever was around would become part of me or I would become part of it: be it darkness, or sky, or tree, or wind. Words would flash in my inner darkness, I would follow them, it would be like a game, sometimes I would catch them, sometimes they would catch me. (ibid., p.20)

This intensity of experience, a sense of mystical communion with nature, the 'desire to discover by becoming the thing' (ibid., p.35) is characteristic of 'About being this way' (included here) and in much of Milan's writing. Nature and poetry heal the wounds of the suffering woman; they are her refuge, her sustenance. This merging with nature, the disappearing of boundaries, the erasure of the Self in her poetry are reminiscent of the 'oneness' postulated in the Upanishads. She yearns for aloneness where 'there is nothing, to such an extent that one's being too disappears.' (ibid., p.34)

Jyotsna Milan has not published much. The relentless critic inside her convicts much of her writing to life-imprisonment in her many notebooks. More importantly, her duties as a wife and a mother, and her work for SEWA do not leave her much time for writing. But her slim volumes are a rich testimony to woman's experience: to her pain, oppression, suffocation, loneliness, deprivation, but also to her invincible soul.

The text of the poems is from Milan 1989 and Apne āge āge. Translations of her poetry have been published in Zide 1993, pp.131–2; Dharwadker 1996, p.20 and Indian literature 180, pp.24–5. An interview with Jyotsna Milan (Milan 1995) is the only available source of information on her at present.

Jyotsna   Milan

इस तरह होने के बारे में
पहले
पेड़ और मैं
साथ–साथ थे
हमने सोचा ही नहीं कभी
अपने

इस तरह होने के बारे में
हम इसी तरह थे
शुरू से

हमारे इस तरह होने में
हमारी कोई भूमिका नहीं थी

मगर

इससे पहले
कभी पता नहीं चला
कि हमारा
यों साथ–साथ होना
हमारे हो सकना की शर्त है।

About being this way
Before,
tree and I
were together
We never even thought of
our
being this way
We were this way
from the beginning
We played no part
in our being this way
But
previously
we never realised
that our
being together in this way
is the condition for our being

आसमान

बैठी रही
साल-दर-साल
अपने ही भीतर
देखती रही
खिड़की के पार
आसमान को
घुस आया एक दिन
कमरे में
बोला, उड़ो
घूम-घूमकर देखती रही वह
आसमान को
जो घर के बाहर भी था
और भीतर भी ।

Sky

She sat
year after year
inside her own self
Kept looking
through the window
at the sky
One day it entered
the room
and said, Fly!
Turning round she kept looking
at the sky
which was both outside the house
and inside.

लगातार

एकाएक
अपने पैरों को देखा
तो भर उठी दहशत से
बरसों पहले
जहाँ गाड़ा गया था
वहीं खड़ी थी मैं
जिसका
जो मन आया
टाँगता चला गया
थैला, टोपी, अँगोछा

या
अपनी थकान
और लगता रहा सारे वक्त
कि मैं
चलती रही हूँ
लगातार ।

Constantly

Suddenly
I looked at my feet
and
was filled with dread--
I was still standing
where years ago
I had been planted
Everybody
hung on me
whatever they fancied--
a bag, a hat, a towel
or their tiredness
And it seemed to me
that all this while
I was
on the move
constantly

पैर

खड़े थे पैर
असमंजस में
चलें कि खड़े रहें
सोच में पड़ गए वे
चलने से पहले

चट से
उठते थे
और चलने लगते थे
बचपन में
नहीं होती थीं कोई निश्चित बजहें
चलने या खड़े होने की
पैरों ने कभी
कल्पना भी नहीं की थी
कि वे

सोचने लगेंगे
एक दिन ।

Feet

The feet stood
in hesitation–
Should they go or stay?
Lost in thought
before moving

They used to lift
instantly
and start walking
In her childhood
there were no fixed reasons
for going or staying

The feet had never
imagined
that they
would start thinking
one day.

पीछे

चलते-चलते
अचानक ही पलटकर देखा
पीछे
न कोई सड़क थी न मैदान
न वो शहर
न वे घर
न वे जगहें
न वे लोग
जहाँ से वह शुरू हुई थी
कहीं कुछ भी नहीं था पीछे
जैसे
वह जो जीवन जीती गयी
कोई पोंछता चला गया हो
लगे हाथ ।

Behind

Stopping midway
she turned and looked
behind

There was no road, no field
nor the town,
houses,
places,
people
of her birth
No trace of anything
As if
someone had been carefully
wiping out
the life she lived.

तलाश
जलाती है गैस
बनाती है चाय
करती है
घर को साफ़
बदलती है बदरंग चादरें
आते हैं लोग
कहते हैं
'आपका घर
लगता है
सचमुच का एक घर'
देखती है वो
चकित
अपने घर को
घूमती है कमरों में
ढूँढ़ती है एक घर
मिलता है एक कमरा
सोफ़ा-तख्त कुर्सियाँ
एक और कमरा भी
बिस्तर-चटाइयाँ-मशीनें
घेर लेती हैं
तमाम चीज़ें
होती है वह
किसी एक कमरे में
और आत्मा
आवारा भटकती है
घर की तलाश में
जैसे
किसी की न हो ।

Search

She turns the gas on,
makes tea
cleans the house,
changes the faded sheets.
People come
and say,
'Your house
really feels
like home.
Astonished
she looks at
her house
Wanders in the rooms,
looks for a home
Finds a room
sofa bed, chairs,
another room
bed, mats, appliances
All these things enclose
every room where she is
And her soul, astray,
roams about
in search of home
as if it is no ones.

औरत

प्यार के क्षणों मे
कभी-कभी
ईश्वर की तरह लगता है मर्द
औरत को
'ईश्वर . . . ईश्वर . . .'
की पुकार से
दहकने लगता है
उसका समूचा वजूद
अचानक
कहता है मर्द
'देखो
मैं ईश्वर हूँ'
औरत
ईश्वर को खो देने की पीड़ा से बिलबिलाकर
फेर लेती है
अपना मुँह ।

Woman

In moments of love
sometimes
man seems like God
to the woman
The cry
'God . . . God. . .'
sets her whole being
aflame
Suddenly
he says,
'Look
I am God'
She
looks at him
and
pained by the loss of God
turns
her face away

शब्द

आँख मूँदकर
घुमाती है पेन्सिल,
खींचती है एक लकीर
घिर आता है
भीतर
कितना सारा शून्य
ढूँढती है वह
एक शब्द
समूची भाषा में
उसके ख़िलाफ़ ।

Words

She closes her eyes
and moving the pencil round
draws a line
How much void
is encircled
within?
She seeks for
a single word
in the entire language
to fight it.

अर्थ

रोटी के
उस दुःख से
कभी साबका नहीं पड़ा
जब जीवन का
रोटी के अलावा
कोई अर्थ नहीं बचता
उस दुःख को थोड़ा सा जानती हूँ
जब शरीर में पगी आत्मा
उधड़ने लगती है
और जब जूझते हुए शरीर के लिए
रोटी का भी
कोई अर्थ नहीं बचता ।

Meaning

I have never experienced
the grief
of the bread
when
life has no meaning,
but bread.
I know that grief a little
when the soul steeped in the body
becomes undone
and when for the struggling body
even bread
loses its meaning.

रात

सबसे पहले
शुरू होता है माँ का दिन
मुँह अँधेरे
और सब के बाद तक
चलता है
छोटी होती हैं
माँ की रातें नियम से
और दिन
नियम से लंबे
रात में दूर तक धँसे हुए
इसे कोई भी
दिन की घुसपैठ नहीं मानता

माँ की रात में
पैर सिकोड़कर
रोज़ सोती है
गुड़ी-मुड़ी माँ
बची-खुची रात में
पैर फैलाने लायक
लँबी भी नही होती
माँ की रात ।

Night

A mother's day begins
first
at the crack of dawn
It ends
last
Mother's nights
are always short
Her days
always long,
stealing into the night

Nobody considers this
to be a day's trespassing
into the mother's night

Everyday she sleeps
with legs drawn in—
A crumpled mother
in the left-over night

Mother's night
is not long enough
even to stretch out.

साथ-साथ आइने में

इस तरफ़ थी वह
दरवाज़े के
साथ-साथ आइने में झाँकते
मकान और आसमान
उस तरफ़

अंतहीन उजले आसमान में
धमकी की तरह
अँधेरा एक
इकलौता मकान ।

Together in the mirror

She was on this side
of the door

On that side
Peeping into the mirror together,
house and sky

In the boundless radiant sky
a single
dark house
Like a threat.

किसी दूसरी जगह

पहले ही
दूर चली गई
घर से
किसी दूसरी जगह जाने की तरह
कि लौट आए
घर लौटने की तरह ।

Some other place

She went far
from home
as if going to some other place
So that she might return
as if returning home.

वह

अपने केशों को
वस्त्र की तरह पहने
बैठी थी
घुटनों पर हाथ बांधे
अपनी ही बाँहों से घिरी ।

She

Wearing her tresses
like a garment,
she was sitting–
hands joined on her knees–
embraced by her own arms.

GLOSSARY

AGYEYA

दूर्वाचल

दूर्वाचल m. verdant hill (दूर्वा grass + अचल
    mountain)
पार्श्व m. side, flank
गिरि m. mountain: hill
नम्र adj. bent, bowed
चीड़ f. pine or fir tree
डगर f. path
उमंग f. height of feeling, rapture
बिछना vi. to be spread out, laid
पैर m. foot
नदी f. river
रेखा f. contour, outline
विहग m. bird
शिशु m. the young of an animal
मौन adj. silent
नीड़ m. nest
दिलासा m. inv. consolation.
    ~ देना:(को) to console
पुन: adv. again
भले ही adv. even if
अनगिन adj. countless
क्षितिज m. horizon
पलक f. eyelid
तमकना vi. to flush with anger
दामिनी f. lightning
यायावर m. wanderer

उषा-दर्शन

उषा f. dawn
दर्शन m. seeing, sight; audience
चाँद m. moon
सिहरना vi. to shiver
कुई f. water-lily; white lotus
आक्षितिज adv. up to the horizon
    (आ-up to + क्षितिज horizon)
तम m. darkness
थमना vi. to stand still

जमना vi. to be collected, to gather
लजीला adj. shy, bashful
भोर m. dawn, daybreak
रश्मि f. ray
समाना vi. to be contained or held in, to
    fill
चुपके से adv. quietly, secretly
हिमाहत adj. frost-nipped (हिम frost + आहत
    struck)
नलिनी f. lotus, lily
खिलाना vt. to cause to bloom
प्रगल्भा adj. (f.) conceited
मानमयी f. capricious one
बावला adj. crazy, frenzied

रात में गाँव

झींगुर m. cricket: cicada
लोरी f. lullaby
झोंपड़ा m. hut
हिंडोल m. swing, cradle
झुलाना vt. to rock
धीमे adv. gently
उजला adj. bright, radiant
कपासी adj. made of cotton: cotton-white
धूम m. smoke
डोरी f. string, cord

चुप-चाप

चुप-चाप adv. quietly
झरना vi. to fall
स्वर m. sound: murmur
शरद f. autumn
झील f. lake
लहर f. wave, ripple
तिरना vi. to float
रहस्य m. mystery, secret
ठहरना vi. to be fixed, still
गहराना vi. to deepen
पुलकित adj. ecstatic, enraptured
विराट् adj. & m. vast: expanse

शिशिर का भोर

शिशिर m. the cold season
भोर m. daybreak, dawn
प्रकाश m. light, daylight
सन्नाटा m. dead silence

नन्दा देवी १४

निचले adv. below
शिखर m. summit
देवल m. shrine
निराकार adj. & m. formless; the ultimate
  being

असाध्य वीणा

असाध्य adj. unmastered, indomitable
वीणा f. veena, Indian lute
सहसा adv. suddenly
झनझनाना vi. to resound
संगीतकार m. musician
पिघलना vi. to melt. → पिघली liquid
ज्वाला f. blaze
झलकना vi. to shine; to flash
रोमांच m. thrill
बिजली f. lightning
तन m. body
अवतरित adj. descended
स्वयंभू m. the self-existent–title of
  Brahma, Vishnu or Shiva
अखण्ड adj. unbroken
मौन m. silence
अशेष adj. infinite
प्रभामय adj. radiant, lustrous
डूबना vi. to be immersed
एकाकी adj. alone, separate
पार adv. across
तिरना vi. to cross over, to float
जय f. victory
यशःकाय adj. fame-bodied (यशस् fame +
  काय body)
वरमाल f. garland
मंगल adj. auspicious
दुन्दुभी m. large drum
राज-मुकुट royal crown
सिरिस m. mimosa
महदाकांक्षा f. great ambition
  (महत great + आकांक्ष ambition)

द्वेष m. hatred, aversion
चाटु m. flattery
लुगड़ा m. ragged cloth
झरना vi. to be shed
निखरना vi. to be purified
कांचन m. gold
धर्म m. duty
भाव m. feeling; manner
निछावर f./m. sacrifice
छँटना vi. to be scattered
बदली f. small cloud
कौंध f. flash (as of lightning), sudden
  dazzling light
मणि f./m. jewel
माणक m. ruby; jewel
कंठहार m. necklace
पट m. garment
वस्त्र m. cloth, material
मेखला f. girdle
किंकिणि f. small bell; belt of small bells
अंधकार m. darkness
कण m. particle, fragment
आलोक m. light
अनन्य adj. single, undivided
विद्युल्लता f. flash of lightning
घेरना vt. to surround, to encircle: to
  entwine
रस m. pleasure, joy
भार m. load: amass
मेघ m. cloud
थिरकना vi. to move in delicate or
  expressive way: to swing
छिपना vi. to be hidden
आश्वस्त adj. reassured
सहज m. natural: pure
विश्वास m. trust, reliance
साधना vt. to practise, to achieve by
  devotion: to strive for
कृपा f. grace, mercy
वाक्य m. utterance
प्रभु m. God
आतंक m. fear, terror
मुक्ति f. release; freedom
आश्वासन m. assurance, reassurance
तिजोरी f. safe
सोना m. gold
खनक f. ringing, jingling
बटुली f. small cooking-pot

अन्न m. food, provisions
सौंधा adj. fragrant: delicious
ख़ुशबू f. fragrance
वधू f. bride, young wife
सहमा adj. timid
पायल m. ankle bells
ध्वनि f. sound: tinkle
शिशु m. infant, young child
किलकारी m. shouting aloud
    (in excitement or in delight)
जाल m. net
फँसना vi. to be caught
तड़पन f. writhing: thrashing
अपर adj. other, another
चहक f. warbling, chirping
मुक्त adj. free
नभ m. sky, heavens: infinite
उड़ना vi. to fly, to soar
मण्डी f. market
ठेलमठेल f. shoving, jostling
गाहक m. customer
आस्पर्धा f. rivalry, scramble
ताल-युक्त adj. rhythmical
घण्टा m. bell, chime
लोहा m. iron, steel: anvil
सधना vi. to be made, completed
हथौड़ा m. heavy hammer
सम adj. even, steady
चोट f. blow
लंगर m. anchor
कसमसाना vi. to stir, to be agitated, to
    fidget: to chafe
नौका f. boat
लहर f. wave
अविराम adj. ceaseless
थपक f. pat, tap
बटिया f. narrow path
चमरौधा m. heavy country-made shoe
रूँधना vi. to be confined
चाप f. (the sound of) footsteps
कुलिया f. channel, stream
मेड़ f. dike, embankment
बहना vi. to flow, to overflow: to stream
जल m. water
छुल-छुल f. dribble; gurgle
गमक f. deep tone or sound; trill
    (in music): tinkle
नर्तिन f. dancer

एड़ी f. heel
घुँघरू m. string of small bells worn around
    the ankles
युद्ध m. battle
ढोल m. large drum: thunder
संझा f. evening, twilight
गोधूली f. dust, twilight
लघु adj. weak, light: gentle
टुन-टुन f. ringing, clanging: chime
प्रलय m. dissolution of the world at the
    end of an age: doom
डमरू m. small drum
नाद m. loud noise: beat
अँगडाई f. twisting or stretching the limbs:
    langour
महाजृम्भ m. great yawn
विकराल adj. hideous
काल m. time; fate; death
तिरना vi. to float: to drift
झिपना vi. to be closed; to be hidden: to
    be immersed
जागना vi. to wake up: to be roused
वशंवद adj. subject to, dominated by:
    subdued
स्तब्ध adj. dumbfounded
इयत्ता f. scope, extent: self
संधीत = संधित ? adj. joined, united
विलय m. merging; dissolving
मूक adj. silent, mute

जो पुल बनायेंगे

पुल m. bridge
अनिवार्यतः adv. inevitably
सेना f. army, force
पार होना to cross over
जयी adj. victorious
निर्माता m. inv. maker; builder
इतिहास m. history
बन्दर m. monkey
कहलाना vi. to be called

काले मेग्दान

परकोटा m. fortified wall, rampart
खाई f. ditch, trench, moat
ढंग से adv. properly, carefully
सँवरना vi. to be arranged, ordered

महायुद्ध m. great war

हथियार m. weapon

रूँडा adj. headless, just with torso

टुण्डा adj. mutilated

तोप f. cannon

नकचिपटा adj. flat-nosed

गोला-फेंक m. mortar (weapon)

पपोटा m. eyelid

रहित adj. devoid of

अंधा adj. blind

ताकना vt. to stare

आकाश m. sky

टिला m. mound

बेढंगा adj. disorderly

झंखाड़ m. dense thicket

अधढँका adj. half-covered: overgrown

मठ m. religious establishment

गिरिजाघर m. church

खँडहर m. ruin

चौकाठ = चौखट f. frame

उमड़ना vi. to rise; to surge

अँधियारा m. darkness

मनुष्य m. human being, man

मानो conj. as if

खोजना vt. to search, to seek

धरती f. earth

ईश्वर m. God

हत्यारा m. murderer, assassin

नरक की समस्या

नरक m. hell

सो pron. = वह

MUKTIBODH

अंधेरे में

चक्कर लगाना vt. to pace up and quad down, to circle about

पैर m. foot, footstep

तिलिस्मी adj. enchanted

खोह f. cave

गिरफ्तार adj. arrested, seized

भीत f. wall, partition

पार m. & adv. (on, or to) the far bank or side; across

गहन adj. deep

रहस्यमय adj. mysterious

अंधकार m. darkness

ध्वनि f. echo; sound

अस्तित्व m. existence

जनाना vt. to cause to be known: to assert

अनिवार adj. not to be warded off; unstoppable?

हृदय m. heart

धक-धक f. beating, palpitation

अकस्मात adv. suddenly

फूलना vi. to swell, to bulge

खिरना = खिलना vi. to crack

चूना m. lime, slaked lime

रेत f. sand

खिसकना vi. to slip

पपड़ी f. flake

खुद-ब-खुद adv. of its own accord

स्वयमपि adv. of its own accord

मुख m. silhouette, face

दिवाल = दीवार f. wall

नुकीला adj. pointed

भव्य adj. magnificent, splendid

ललाट m. brow

दृढ़ adj. firm

हनु f. chin

अनजाना adj. unknown

आकृति f. form, shape

अभिव्यक्ति f. expression

पूर्ण adj. full; whole

अवस्था f. state, condition

निज adj. one's own

संभावना f. capacity: potential

निहित adj. latent, contained

प्रभा f. light, radiance: brilliance

प्रतिभा f. brilliance, talent

परिपूर्ण adj. complete

आविर्भव m. appearance, manifestation: realisation

रिसना vi. to ooze

तनाव m. tension

आत्मा f. soul

प्रतिमा f. image

सूना adj. empty

राह f. road

फैलाव m. expanse

सर्द adj. cold

ढीला adj. indifferent

उदास adj. sad

तारा m. star

सोच f. reflection, concern

बढ़ना vi. to grow

अँधियारा adj. & m. dark

निःसगं adj. unattached; indifferent: careless

लहर f. wave

काँपना vi. to tremble: to vibrate

टकराना vi. to collide: to clash

सियार m. jackal

ध्वनि f. noise: howling

दूरी f. distance

गूँजना vi. to echo

फ़ासला m. intervening space, interspace

चीख़ना vi. to scream

पक्षी m. bird

द्वार m. door

ख़ोजना vt. to search for

शोध m. investigation; research ~ करना to examine

पूर्णतम adj. absolute (पूर्ण complete + - तम suffix which forms superlatives)

परम adj. highest, ultimate

पलातक adj. fugitive

जगत् m. world, universe

गली f. lane, alley

प्रति adj. every

पल m. moment

फटे हाल in tatters

रूप m. appearance; manner

विघुल्लहरिल adj. of lightning-wave (विघुत् lightning + लहरिल wavy) ?

गतिमयता f. speediness

उद्विग्न adj. anxious

सकर्मक adj. active: vigorous

अतिशयता f. abundance

अविरत adj. incessant, ceaseless

जग = जगत्

झाँकना vi. to peep, to spy

प्रत्येक adv. each, every

गतिविधि f. activity, action

चरित्र m. conduct, account of person's life: deeds

इतिहास m. history

राजनीतिक adj. political

स्थिति f. situation

परिवेश m. circumstance

मानवीय adj. human

स्वानुभूत adj. self-perceived

आदर्श m. ideal

विवेक m. discrimination

प्रक्रिया f. process

कियागत adj. active

परिणति m. transformation

पठार m. plateau

आत्म-संभवा adj. (f.) self-born

चाँद का मुँह टेढ़ा है

टेढ़ा adj. crooked

बीचोबीच m. & adv. the very middle, midst

स्याह adj. black

शिला f. rock

दिवाल = दीवार f. wall

घेरा m. fence, enclosure

अहाता m. enclosed space

काँच m. glass

टुकड़ा m. fragment

जमना vi. to be fixed

सिरा m. edge, end

सँवलाई adj. dark-complexioned: inky ?

झालर f. fringe, frill

कलमुँहा adj. & m. black-faced

मीनार f./m. minaret

उद्गार m. expression of strong feeling

चिह्नाकार m. the shape of sign or mark (चिह्न mark, sign + आकार shape, form)

लटकना vi. to be hanging, suspended

खटक m. apprehension

रे interj. expression of contempt, astonishment or sorrow

गगन m. sky

धरती f. earth

चुपचाप adj. silent

जहरीला adj. poisonous

छी interj. expression of disgust

थू interj. the sound of spitting, shame!

सुनसान adj. desolate

घोसला m. nest

पैठना vi. to penetrate

कारतूस m. cartridge

छर्रा m. charge of shot

हवेली f. mansion

सिहरना vi. to shiver, to shudder

गंजा adj. bald

किरन f./m. ray

जासूस m. spy

साम-सूम adj. black-skied (साम black + सुम sky) ?

घूमना-घामना vi. to wander about

तिकोना m. triangle

छुपना vi. to hide, to be hidden

महसूस करना vt. to feel

कनखी f. side-glance

छानना vt. to search closely

आडा adj. diagonal, oblique

तिरछा adj. diagonal

काटना vt. to cut

पीला adj. pale

पट्टी f. strip

बिछाना vt. to spread out

समीप adj. near

विशालाकार adj. monstrous

   (विशाल huge + आकार size)

अँधियाला adj. dark

ताल m. tank, pond

सूनेपन m. emptiness, void

स्याही f. blackness

डूबना vi. to sink

सँवलाई adj. dark ?

पुल m. bridge

महराब = मेहराब f. arch

सिमटना vi. to be drawn together, to contract → सिमटी jammed

बस्ती f. settlement

बहना vi. to flow

अटकना vi. to be stopped

झरना vi. to flow

पथरीला adj. gravelly, gritty

नाला m. drain, gutter

धार f. current

धराशायी adj. resting on the earth; fallen to the ground

हरिजन m. outcaste, untouchable

कबीठ m. the wood-apple

धड़ m. trunk of tree

मटमैला adj. dirty

छप्पर m. thatched roof

बरगद m. the banyan tree

ऐंठना vi. to be twisted, coiled

अभरना vi. to swell

जड़ f. root

कुहासा m. fog

लटकना vi. to hang

चूनर-चुनरी f. part-coloured cloth sheet or saree

चिथरा = चिथडा m. rag, tatter

अँगिया f. bodice

घाघरा m. skirt

व्यभिचारी adj. vicious

टक टकी f. fixed stare

कंजा adj. having light-coloured eyes

अजी interj. expression of astonishment or disapproval

मसखरी f. clown, buffoon

तिमंजिला adj. three-storeyed

धब्बा m. blot, stain, spot

चमकना vi. to shine, to glare

समेटना vt. to gather up: to fold

ताक f. watch, lookout

चढना vi. to climb

छत f. ceiling

खपरैल m. tiled roof

शाख f. branch

सहायता f. help, assistance

आँगन m. courtyard

गुंबद m. cupola

महल m. mansion

उलाँघना vt. to jump over

गुहा f. cave; secret place: den

दबे-पाँव adv. stealthily

खुफिया adj. inv. secret

सुराग m. search

गुप्तचरी f. espionage, spying

चिपकाना vt. to stick

भडकीला adj. showy flashy

वर्ण m. form, shape

बाँका adj. crooked: slanting

घनघोर adj. fearsome

कोलतारी adj. made of coal tar

घुग्घू m. owl

गला फाडना to make oneself hoarse with shouting

हिचकी f. hiccup

ताल m./f. (music) beating time

खंभा m. pillar, pole

थमना vi. to be held, supported

सट्टा m. commercial transaction

सुर m. sound

भर्राना vi, to become hoarse:
  to croak

झनझनाना vi. to rattle, jingle

कनटोप m. cap with flaps that cover
  ears

संकट m. crisis, danger

गुनगुनाना vi. to mutter

सचाई f. truth

अधजला adj. half-burnt

मुर्दा = मुरदा m. dead body

चिता f. funeral pyre

अधफूटा adj. flaring (अध -half + फूटना to
  explode)

दहक f. tongue of flame

अकस्मात् adv. suddenly

थरथराना vi. to tremble

प्रकाश m. light

चिथड़ा m. tatter, rag

बिंब m. shadow

क्षेप m. throw, cast

अफ़सोस m. regret, sorrow

गहरा adj. grave

दुखड़ा m. suffering, woe

अति adj. very much, excessive

संस्कृत adj. refined, cultured

गोल adj. round

मटका m. large earthen pot

नम्रता f. softness

घिघियाना vi. to whine

स्वर m. voice

स्तूप m. Buddhist monument

मानव m. mankind

गड़ना vi. to be buried

गाड़ना vt. to bury

ईसा m. Jesus

पंख m. wing

झड़ना vi. to be shed

झाड़ना vt. to cause to fall; to shake off: to
  be torn away

सत्य m. truth

देवदासी f. dancing-girl, temple prostitute

उधाड़ना vt. to extricate: to strip off

आँत f. bowels, intestines

चीरना vt. to split, to cut

फाड़ना vt. to tear open

खोल m. hollow, cavity

झोल m. sac, womb: cavity

बेचैन चील

बेचैन adj. restless

चील f. kite

पर्यटनशील adj. roaming

दमकना vi. to glitter

झील f. lake

कोरा adj. mere

झाँसा m. deception: mirage

चिलचिलाहट f. blaze

सूना adj. blank

SHAMSHER

एक पीली शाम

पतझर m. fall of leaves, autumn

अटकना vi. to linger

पत्ता m. leaf

भावना f. emotion; thought

मुखकमल m. lotus face (मुख face
  + कमल lotus)

कृश adj. emaciated; fine

म्लान adj. dejected

हारना vt. to lose

मौन adj. silent, still

दर्पण m. mirror

वासना f. desire

शिथिल adj. languid, weary

पल m. moment

स्नेह m. affection

काजल m. kohl

अद्भुत adj. wonderful, wondrous

रूप m. shape; beauty

कोमलता f. softness

आँसू m. tear

साँध्य adj. having to do with twilight

तारक m. star

अतल adj. & m. unfathomable

उषा

उषा f. dawn

प्रात m. & adv. (in the) early morning,
  (at) dawn

नभ m. sky, heavens

शंख m. conch shell

भोर f./m. daybreak

राख f. ashes

लीपना vt. to smear
चौका m. cooking or eating area
गीला adj. wet
सिल f. stone (for grinding spices)
केसर m. saffron
खड़िया f. chalk
चाक m. slit, crack: streak
मलना vt. to crush, to grind
जल m. water
गौर adj. fair
झिलमिल adj. glistening
देह f. body
हिलना vi. to sway
जादू m. spell, enchantment
सूर्योदय m. sunrise

पूर्णिमा का चाँद

पूर्णिमा f. the night or day of
    full moon
चाँद m. moon
बादल m. cloud
गलना vi. to dissolve
आसमान m. sky, heavens
दरिया m. inv. river
उमड़ना vi. to swell, to rise
गुलाब m. rose :
चूमना vt. to kiss
झिलमिलाना vi. to shimmer
स्वप्न m. dream

सु ब ह

सिकुड़ना vi. to shrivel, to shrink
पत्थर m. stone
सजग adj. alert; awake
पसरना vi. to be stretched out

धूप कोठरी के आइने में खड़ी

धूप f. sunlight
कोठरी f. small room; hut
आइन = आईना m. mirror
पारदर्शी adj. transparent, translucent
पर्दा = परदा m. a blind
मौन adj. silent
आँगन m. courtyard
मोम m. wax
कोमल adj. soft, delicate

नभ m. sky, heavens
मधुमक्खी f. honey bee
हिलाना vt. to sway
नन्हा adj. tiny, young
उड़ना vi. to take flight
उदास adj. sad
मा=माँ f. mother
मुख m. face

प्रेयसी

प्रेयसी f. beloved
प्रेमिका f. beloved
आइना = आईना m. mirror
बदन m. body
माध्यम m. means
प्यारी f. & adj. (f.) beloved; dear, precious
काँसा m. bronze
चिकना adj. smooth, sleek
हिलना vi. to swing, to stir
हौले adv. softly, slowly
नाचना vi. to dance
स्थिर adj. unmoving; lasting
रूप m. manner, mode
साकार adj. having form or shape;
    incarnate
अनजाना adj. unknown; strange
कायनात f. world, universe
गंदुमी adj. wheat-coloured
गुलाब m. rose
पाँखुड़ी f. petal
शबनम f. dew
चारों तरफ adv. all around
घुलना vi. to melt
सुडौल adj. graceful
आबशार m. waterfall, fountain
गतिमान adj. dynamic; agile
मूर्त adj. tangible
उज्ज्वल adj. radiant
ढलना vi. to be cast
गोलाई f. curvature, curve
सीना m. chest
कसना vt. to draw tight; to press against
सादा adj. pure, smooth
भीना adj. light
ठोस adj. solid; dense: sculpted
अजब तौर से adv. in a strange way:
    wondrously
वसना to dwell, reside

तुमने मुझे

गूँगा adj. mute
सुनहरा adj. golden
आभा f. gleam
छाना vi. to be diffused
गहरा m. depth
गार m. cave, cavern
चारों तरफ adv. all around
नदी f. river
लहर f. wave, ripple
हजरत m. Sir; title for eminent persons:
    Mr/ Miss
आदम m. Adam
यौवन m. youth
बचपना m. childishness
हौव्वा f. Eve
युवा adj. young
मासूमियत f. innocence
लिपटना vi. to be embraced: to be
    enfolded
व्यक्तित्व m. personality, individuality:
    uniqueness
मुख m. mouth
आनंद m. bliss
स्थायी adj. lasting, permanent
ग्रास m. morsel
मूक adj. speechless

कवि घंघोल देता है

कवि m. poet
घंघोलना vt. to stir
व्यक्ति m. person, individual
जल m. water: streams; lakes
हिला-मिलाना vt. to mix
दर्पन=दर्पण m. mirror
दर्शन m. sight
गंभीर adj. profound
अंत m. end

RAGHUVIR SAHAY

आज फिर

सरल adj. simple
सूरज m. sun
शीतल adj. cool, refreshing
जल m. water

जी भर adv. to one's heart's content
किलकना vi. to shout or cry out loud (in
    delight, or excitement)
चढ़ना vi. to climb, to mount
आदि m. beginning
गान m. singing

पानी के संस्मरण

संस्मरण m. reminiscences, memories
कौंध f. flash, sudden dazzle of light
घोर m. deep, dense
वन m. forest, jungle
मूसलाधार adj. torrential, heavy (rain)
वृष्टि f. rain
घना adj. massed, full: brimful
ताल m. pond
झुकना vi. to be bent down
डाल f. branch
बयार m. cool wind
फुहार f. fine rain, drizzle
उजला adj. shimmering, shining
रेती f. sand-bank
के पार ppn. across
गहरा adj. deep

वसन्त

वसन्त m. spring
आदर्श adj. ideal: classic
मन m. heart
अनुभव m. experience, feeling

मैदान में

मैदाम m. flat, open field, plain
चाँदना m. moonlight, light
गोरा adj. fair-complexioned
लुनाई f. beauty, savour, charm
डबडबाना vi. to overflow, to brim
केश m. hair
सूना adj. desolate, ruined
दिशा f. direction; region: space
गति f. movement, course
ठिठकना vi. to stand still
रोशनी f. light

सेब बेचना

डपटना vt. to rebuke, to tell off

दाग़ी adj. marked; specked
निश्चिंत adj. free from care
खाँसी f. cough
दौरा m. fit, attack
सीना m. chest
थामना vt. to clutch, seize

अकेली औरत

रोग m. illness
एकांत m. seclusion

मनुष्य-मछली युद्ध

मनुष्य m. human being, man
युद्ध m. war
मीठा पानी fresh water
नाव f. boat, ship
विकराल adj. monstrous
नदी f. river
समाना vi. to fit (into)
डब्बा m. tin, box
लोकतंत्र m. democracy
प्रतीक m. symbol
उपलब्ध adj. available
विज्ञान m. science
जीतना vt. to conquer
विधि f. method, way
आविष्कार m. invention
आँकडा m. statistics
अदम्य adj. irrepressible
इच्छा f. will, urge, desire
नस्ल f. stock, breed
तगडा adj. sturdy
स्वादू adj. delicious, tasty
ताकत से adv. energetically
तड़पना vi. to writhe
नतीजा m. result, conclusion

व्यावहारिक लोग

व्यावहारिक adj. practical
फूलगोभी f. cauliflower
वाह interj. splendid! wonderful!
नरम adj. tender
नीरस adj. bland, uninteresting
सुन्दरी f. beautiful woman
अदलबदल m. exchange
ऊलजलूल adj. silly, stupid

मुनफ़ख़ोर m. profiteer
सभ्यता f. civilisation, society
मनोरंजन m. entertainment
सरकाना vt. to move to one side or out of the way
व्यापारी adj. having to do with business
व्यवस्था f. system, state of affairs

फूट

फूट f. split; rift
असमिया m. Assamese
पिछडा adj. backward
अगडा adj. forward

SAXENA

पाचँ नगर प्रतीक

प्रतीक m. emblem, symbol
कच्चा adj. not fast (dye)
रंग m. colour
नफ़ीस adj. exquisite
चित्रकारी f. decoration
डिबिया f. miniature box, casket
नकली adj. artificial
हीरा m. diamond
अँगूठी f. ring
लिपटना vi. to wrap (around, में)
शृंगारदान m. make-up case
इत्र m. perfume
शीशी f. flask, small bottle
महज़ adv. nothing but, merely
सड़ना vi. to decay, to rot
तागा m. thread
बँधना vi. to be bound, tied
तावीज़ m. amulet
भाँग m. cannabis
छूछा adj. empty
गंगाजली f. container for Ganges water.
~ उठाना to swear by the water of the Ganges
कला f. art
पनवाडी m. betel-seller
शीशा m. mirror
धूल f. dust
जमना vi. to settle
अक्स m. reflection

रात में वर्षा

वर्षा f. rain
साँस f. breath
मेघ m. cloud
आकाश m. sky, heavens
पलक f. eyelid
झुकना vi. to be lowered
क्षितिज m. horizon
भुजा f. arm
टकराना vi. to collide (with)
शीशा m. glass
बादल m. cloud
रंग-बिरंग adj. colourful
असंख्य adj. countless
सागर m. ocean, sea
भरना vt. to fill
बौछार f. heavy shower
बूँद f. drop
रंगीन adj. colourful
उड़ना vi. to soar, to take flight
धार f. stream; heavy shower
चढ़ना vi. to climb (on पर)
उतरना vi. to come down
झकोरा m. heavy shower, torrent
हाँफना vi. to gasp, to pant
रोम m. body-hair; pore
पुलक m. thrill of rapture
आकार m. shape, form

अकेलापन

अकेलापन m. loneliness
सूना adj. empty; desolate
टहनी f. small branch, twig
टुकड़ा m. piece टुकड़े करना to break, to split
पास-पास adv. side-by-side

दरवाज़े बंद हैं

स्मृति f. memory
दरार f. crack
रोशनी f. light
खामोशी f. quietness, silence
पसली f. rib
उभरना vi. to rise
नथुना m. nostril
दिमाग m. brain

रेंगना vi. to creep
गंध f. smell
कैद f. imprisonment
फाँदना vt. to jump over
भीतर adv. inside, within
सफेदी f. whiteness; whitewash
कसमसाना vi. to wriggle, to be agitated
धूल f. dust
जमना vi. to settle (as dust)
सूई f. hand (of clock)
हिलाना vt. to move
परित्यक्त adj. abandoned
घोंसला m. nest
कालीन f. carpet
चींटी f. ant

जंगल का दर्द

खामोश adj. quiet, silent
झीना adj. thin, worn
अहिंसक adj. non-violent
सुर्ख adj. red
हिंसक adj. violent, ferocious
पशु m. animal, beast
खूँख्वार adj. bloodthirsty
टुकड़ा m. scrap
फेंकना vt. to throw, to hurl
आहार m. food
गुँथना vi. to be plaited, interlocked: tangled
लहुलुहान adj. smeared with blood
ताकतवर adv. strong, powerful
कमज़ोर adj. weak, feeble
उच्छिष्ट m. leftover food
संतोष m. contentment; resignation
छिपाना vt. to hide
क्रम m. sequence
दर्प m. arrogance
जगाना vt. to awaken, to arouse
आदी होना vi. to be or become accustomed, used
प्रतीक्षा f. waiting
शिकार m. victim, prey

कुआनो नदी

नदी f. river
पसरना vi. to be stretched out

ज़िला m. administrative district
बस्ती a district in U.P.
कूदना vi. to jump
तट m. bank of river
रेत f. sand
सीपी f. shell
सख्त adj. hard, harsh
कँकरीला adj. stony, gravelly
काई f. scum on stagnant water
दलदल f./m. marshy land, swamp
झाड़ी f. undergrowth
सोता m. stream
कुलबुलाना vi. to be restless
टहनी f. small branch, twig
झूलना vi. to swing, to dangle
मुर्दघाट m. burning ghat (मुर्दा dead body
    + घाट river bank)
फूँकना vt. to burn
शव-यात्रा f. funeral procession
शौक m. fondness, hobby
आधी रात f. midnight
गीला adj. damp, wet
अभागा m. unfortunate
चिता f. funeral pyre
मेला m. fair ~ लगना fair to be held
पूर्णिमा f. night or day of full moon
स्नान m. bathing
अहदी m. idle fellow
काम आना vi. to be of use (to के)
दालान m. hallway, corridor
कोना m. corner, quiet place
जाला m. cobweb
ढोल m. large drum
टँगना vi. to hang
बजना vi. to resound
खड़खड़ाना vi. to rustle
विशाल adj. huge, gigantic
झीना adj. worn, wasted
पीपल m. the pipal or holy fig tree
दैवी adj. divine
स्पर्श m. touch
जालीदार adj. netted
प्रतीक्षा करना vt. to wait (for, की)
धूप f. sunlight
गंदगी f. dirt, filth
आवारा adj. stray, vagrant
गुनगुनाना vi. to hum
लिपटना vi. to cling

ग्राहक m. customer
कत्ल m. murder, carnage
लाश f. dead body
फेंकना vt. to discard, to throw
जनमना vi. to be born
जिन्दा adj. inv. alive
रोशनी f. light
गश्त f. patrolling ~ लगाना to go one's
    rounds, to patrol
सियार m. jackal
हुआँ-हुआँ m. howling
चमगादड़ m. bat
शाख f. branch
लपट f. flame
दहकना vi. to blaze, to burn
अंगारा m. cinder, burning matter
आसमान m. sky
तारा m. star
चुपचाप adv. silently
बहना vi. to flow

KUNWAR NARAIN

कमरे में धूप

धूप f. sunshine, sunlight
बहस f. argument, debate
चुपचाप adv. silently, quietly
किरण f. ray, sunbeam
ऊन f. wool
बुनना vt. to knit, to weave
सहसा adv. suddenly
तड़ m. sound of striking, slapping
थप्पड़ m. slap
जड़ना vt. to deliver (a slap)
बाना vi. to be wide open → मुँह बाये
    adv. agape
सुराही f. long-necked jar, jug
छूटना vi. to be let go
कुहराम m. weeping and wailing
खामोशी f. calm, quietness
अँगड़ाई f. twisting or stretching of the
    limbs (as through fatigue) ~ लेना to
    twist or stretch
न जाने who knows

अन्तिम ऊँचाई

अन्तिम adj. last, final

ऊँचाई f. height, altitude: ascent
स्पष्ट adj. clear, distinct
बढ़ना vi. to go forward or ahead
दिशा f. direction, course
के चारों ओर ppn. all around
रूकना iv. to stop, to be still
ऊलजलूल adj. absurd
बेहद adj. without bounds or limits:
    endlessly
हिम्मत f. courage, spirit ~ हारना to lose
    heart
दिलचस्पी f. interest
समास adj. ended
धूमधाम m. display, ostentation
दुर्गम adj. inaccessible, dense
वन m. jungle, scrub-land
पर्वत m. mountain, hill
जीतना vt. to conquer, to defeat
अन्तर m. difference
पत्थर m. stone
कठोरता f. harshness, hardness
मस्तक m. forehead, head
तूफ़ान m. storm
झेलना vt. to endure
काँपना vi. to tremble

बाकी कविता

पत्ता m. leaf
भिन्न adj. different, distinct
मृत्यु f. death
चिह्न f. mark
अस्तित्व m. existence
विराम m. pause: full stop
कहीं भी adv. at any point, anyhow

दूर तक

सुगंध m. fragrance
रूप m. form, shape
रंग m. colour
चमक f. glow, brilliance
गोद f. bosom, embrace
ज़मीन f. earth, soil
बादल m. cloud
आकाश m. sky
भरना vt. to fill; to put (an object into
    container or space so as to fill it): to
    take in

फैलना vi. to spread, to expand, to
    reach out

एक संक्षिप्त कालखण्ड में

संक्षिप्त adj. concise: brief
कालखण्ड m. span of time (काल time +
    खण्ड fragment)
ताकत f. power, strength
पिचकना vi. to be deflated
गुब्बारा m. balloon
नक्शा m. map
साँस f. breath
फुलाना vt. to inflate
गुना adj. multiplicative suffix: -fold, times
अनुभव m. feeling
असह्य adj. unbearable
दबाव m. pressure: strain
प्रयत्न m. effort, attempt
भूमिका f. role: nature
अन्य adj. other, different
यथार्थ m. reality
प्रवेश m. enter ~ करना to enter (into, में)
बेचैन adj. restless
चिंता f. concern, thought
हिम्मत f. courage
फूटना vi. to burst
की हद तक adv. to the point of
नष्ट adj. destroyed, doomed
कर्कश adj. sharp, harsh; violent
विस्फोट m. explosion, blast
विरल adj. unusual, rare
ऊँचाई f. height
कल्पना f. imagination: fantasy
मुक्त adj. free, unrestricted

कबूतर और बिल्ली

कबूतर m. pigeon
कंगूरा m. parapet, pinnacle
मानना vt. to suppose: to imagine
जिंदा adj. inv. alive
दुबकी f. the act of crouching, hiding,
    lurking
झपटना vt. to pounce
पंजा m. paw, claw
दबोचना vt. to seize, to clutch
म्याँऊँ f. mewing

टें f. screech
फड़फड़ाना vi. to flutter, to flap
कैद f. imprisonment
हटना vi. to step back
साफ़ adv. clearly

बदलते पोस्टर

ढहना vt. to be ruined, to fall to pieces
ख़ुशरंग adj. bright, colourful
साबुन m. soap
सुन्दरी f. beautiful woman
वनस्पति m. vegetable oil
पनपना vi. to flourish, to thrive
ख़ाद f. manure, fertiliser
लहलहाना vi. to thrive
फ़सल f. crop, harvest
पान m. betel-leaf
मसाला m. spices
सवार adj. mounted (on, na), riding
पग्गड़ adj. wearing a turban
किसान m. farmer, villager
जोड़ना vt. to join
धन m. wealth
वर्षा f. rainfall
संदेशा m. message
धनकुबेर m. man as rich as the god of
    wealth
गुमसुम adj. quiet
उदास adj. sad
ठेका m. piece-work, contract work
ठेके पर adv. by piece-work
भूखों मरना to starve, to die of hunger

प्रेम का रोग

रोग m. disease, illness
मुश्किल f. distress, problem
भरपूर adj. & adv. ful(ly),
    complete(ly), thoroughly
ताकत f. power; ability
दिनोंदिन adv. day by day
क्षीण adj. diminished, reduced
सदी f. century
राज करना to rule (over, पर)
आड़ना vt. to obstruct; get in the way
एहसान m. favour
की कुछ चलना something to succeed for
    someone

छाना vi. to be spread: to appear
झुकना vi. to bend down, to bow
लाख समझाना to counsel over and over
    again
मन m. mind, heart
अपनाना vt. to treat as one's own, to adopt
प्रेमिका f. beloved
धोखा m. deceit
ख़ून m. blood. ~ करना to kill, to murder
घूँट m. mouthful
पागल m. madman, fool
भटकना vi. to wander
जी m. heart, spirit
हल्का adj. light. ~ करना to lighten (as
    burden)
उल्टा adj. & m. contrary
बढ़ना vi. to increase
वहम m. suspicion
पक्का adj. firm
जड़ f. root. ~ पकड़ना to take root
स्वर्ग m. heaven

KEDARNATH SINGH

बाज़ार

धूल f. dust
मिट्टी f. earth, dust
चमक f. sparkle
बेहद adj. limitless, unbounded
सादगी f. simplicity
स्तब्ध adj. stunned, stupefied
आश्चर्य m. amazement

अकाल में सारस

अकाल m. drought, famine
सारस m. the Sarus crane
झुंड m. flock (as of birds)
छाना vt. to cover
आसमान m. sky
क्रेंकार m. bird-cry
सारा का सारा adj. the whole (of)
परिक्रमा f. circumambulation
छत f. roof
बारजा m. upper porch
डैन m. wing
झरना vi. to fall

धान m. rice plant
सूखा adj. dry
पत्ती f. leaf
गंध f. smell
आँगन m. courtyard
बीचोबीच adv. in the very middle
जल m. water
भरा adj. full of
कटोरा m. shallow cup or bowl
दूर-देसावर m. far away; foreign place
गर्दन m. neck
निगाह f. glance
दया f. compassion, pity
घृणा f. aversion, hatred
मुड़ना vi. to turn (back)
पीटना vt. to beat
दूरी f. distance

आना

जाँगर m. bodily energy
धमनी f. vein
रक्त m. blood
चूल्हा m. stove, hearth
आँच f. flame, fire
बबूल m./f. acacia tree
चीरना vt. to split, to tear
फाड़ना vt. to tear, to lacerate
बाद m. promise
धज्जी f. shred, strip. धज्जियाँ उड़ना (की) to
   tear to shreds, to show to be worthless

कुछ और टुकड़े ९

टुकड़ा m. fragment
चुप्पी f. silence
भयानक adj. fearsome
गौंड़ा m. a rhinoceros
सींग m. horn
पास-पास adv. side by side
गर्भ m. womb
चुपचाप adv. silently

सुखी आदमी

सुखी adj. happy, contented
हास्यास्पद adj. ridiculous
धूप f. sun

खिलना vi. to be striking or attractive, to
   be radiant
ठीक -ठाक adv. fine
दुरूस्त adj. in good order, sound (of
   health)
सलाख f. iron bar
आसमान m. sky
फूटकर रोना to shed floods of tears
माँद f. den, lair

बाघ ६

बाघ m. tiger
लोमड़ी f. fox
समर्थन m. confirmation, agreement
हिलाना vt. to nod
एकटक m. fixed gaze → adv. (with देखना)
   steadily, fixedly
जबड़ा m. jaw
खून m. blood
गंध f. smell
तड़पना vi. to be eager
गड़ना vi. to pierce
अबकी adv. this time
आश्चर्य m. surprise
झुकाना vt. to incline (the head)
निरुपाय adj. helpless

मैंने गंगा को देखा

तरसना vi. to suffer (for want of को): to
   thirst for
प्रचंड adj. raging, burning
लू f. hot wind
थपेड़ा m. slap, blow, impact
साहस m. courage, vigour
ताज़गी f. freshness
बेहद adj. unbounded, limitless
रोहू m./f. a kind of large fish
डब-डब f. tearfulness
अपार adj. infinite, shoreless
तरलता f. fluidity
मल्लाह m. boatman
रेती f. sand-bank
वर्ष m. year
उदास adj. sad
शानदार adj. splendid
परछाई f. shadow, reflection

हिलाना vi. to stir, to move
जाल m. net
मुस्कुराना vi. to smile
मुस्कान f. a smile
पछतावा m. regret
सच्चा adj. true, genuine
गहरा adj. deep
कृतज्ञता f. gratitude
बहना vi. to flow
चंचल adj. restless, active
के प्रति ppn. towards
राम-राम interj. & m. form of greeting

SHAKUNT MATHUR

निगाहों ने कहा

निगाह f. look, glance: eyes
भीतर adv. inside
झरना m. waterfall
देवता m. inv. god
घबराहट f. alarm
बढ़ना vi. to grow, to increase
पलक f. eyelid
परी f. fairy
जादुई adj. magic(al)
बाग m. large garden
सीमा f. boundary, limit: end
सरहद f. border; boundary: enclosure

तुम सुन्दर हो, घर सुन्दर हो

चाहे conj. even if
बहना vt. to flow: to pour
पसीना m. sweat
सीना vt. to sew, to stitch
गीला adj. wet
छीलना vt. to peel
तूफ़ान m. storm
जूड़ा m. hair-bun
सजाना vt. to adorn, to decorate
तितली f. butterfly; showily dressed
    woman
वसन m. clothing
नखरा m. flirtatious airs
अधलेटा adj. reclining (अध half + लेटा lying)
शीशा m. mirror: crystal
आहट f. the sound of footsteps

चौंकना vi. to be startled
कविता f. poetry
सलौना adj. charming
प्रियतर adj. dearer: loved (प्रिय dear + -तर
    suffix which forms comparatives)

कॉफ़ी हाऊस

क्षण m. moment, instant
दुःख-सुख m. sorrow and joy
अनिश्चित adj. uncertain
अहसान m. gratitude
पश्चाताप m. remorse; regret
टँगना vi. to be suspended
झाग f./m. foam, froth
मिटना vi. to be erased: to disappear
धार f. stream
सजल adj. full of water
छाँटना vt. to cut, prune
कोमलांगी adj. (f.) lovely, tender (कोमल
    tender + अंग limb)
कुसुम m. flower
शाखा f. branch
लपेटना vt. to wrap, to enfold
पाटना vt. to fill up
ऊष्मा f. heat: fire
गहराई f. depth; abyss
पेय m. any drink
गहरा adj. deep
अतल adj. bottomless
अनडूबा adj. not sunk: floating
घुलना vi. to be dissolved
चूना m. lime

काँच

काँच m. glass; crystal
झटका m. jerk, blow
नज़ाकत f. delicacy, fineness

चुनौती

चुनौती f. challenge
टिक f. direction, space: horizon
मानना vt. to agree, to accept
ढेला m. lump, clod
फेंकना vt. to cast, to throw
घेरना m. to enclose; to confine: to claim
बाँह f. arm, upper arm

पृथ्वी f. earth
भावना f. feeling: passion
जोडना vt. to gather

सहना

सहना vt. to endure, to tolerate
दीवारी f. small wall
ईंट f. brick
कबूतर m. pigeon
कटोरी f. small shallow cup or bowl
समोना vt. to adjust: to settle
भूल f. mistake
आकर्षित adj. attracted
पत्थर m. stone
लांघना vt. to jump, to step over
झरना m. waterfall
चुप्पी f. silence
गगन m. sky
पृथ्वी f. earth
आन्तरिक adj. inner
सूखा adj. dry, withered
खनखन f. tinkling sound: rustle
पुष्प m. flower
पंखुरी f. petal
झरन f. failing
बुझना vi. to be extinguished; to be subdued
अंगार m. spark
अंतर m. interior; heart

छोटी छोटी बातें

नन्हा adj. little, tiny
दृष्टि f. glance
घूरना vt. to stare intently at
झुकना vi. to be bent down
जड f. root
धरती f. earth
कसना vt. to draw tight

चिलका झील

झील f. lake
फैलना vi. to be spread or extended: to be stretched
लोक m. world
छूना vt. to touch

के भीतर ppn. inside
डूबना vi. to sink; to drawn
जागना vi. to wake up
स्थिति f. state, condition
नाव f. boat
गर्भ m. womb
गहरा adj. deep
भाव m. natural state; manner: pose
उन्मादी adj. frenzied
भीषण adj. terrible, fearsome
गर्जन m. the sound of thundering or rumbling: roar
अजदही adj. pertaining to the python
सरकना vi. to move along; to glide (as snake)
बीचोबीच adv. in the middle, or midst
अतिथि m. guest
गृह m. building, room assigned to special purpose
लोक m. people
स्तब्ध adj. startled
हिरन m. deer
झुण्ड m. flock
सन्नाटा m. dead silence
गहराई f. depth, deep

KANTA

धुआँ

वक्ष m. bosom
माथा f. forehead; head
टेकना vt. to lean on: to rest on
सहज adj. unaffected: calm
उचारना vt. to utter
जन्मना vi. to be born
मात्र adj. mere
दुराग्रही adj. excessively stubborn
फैलना vi. to spread
अग्नि f. fire
मरण m. dying, death

सुख

चाहे-अनचाहे wanted or not
सूरजमुखी f. sunflower
तेज adj. strong, fiery; wild
उखडना vi. to become scattered

पीपल m. the pipal or holy fig-tree
ऋन्दन m. lament
स्निग्ध adj. smooth, glossy: shiny
झलमलाना vi. to glitter, sparkle
अकारण adj. causeless, spontaneous
आतुर adj. impatient, restless
दबे पाँव stealthily
अंधकार m. darkness
विवश adj. powerless, helpless
परिताप m. suffering, anguish
गूँगा adj. & m. mute
स्वाद m. taste; relish
अनभिव्यक्त adj. unexpressed
इकतरफा adj. one-sided
अनलौटाया adj. unreturned

डूब गये हैं संकेत

डूबना vi. to sink
संकेत m. indication, hint: trace
गहरा adj. deep, profound
मौन m. silence
अँधकार m. darkness
वाचाल adj. garrulous; boastful

दीवारों पर दीवारें

जीवित adj. alive, living
छूना vt. to touch
छनना vi. to filter
किरन m. ray
जिलाना vt. to give life
पंछी m. bird
फरफराहट f. flutter
बिखेरना vt. to scatter
छत f. ceiling
सटना vi. to join

रोड लैंप का मंदा-मंदा आलोक

मंदा adj, faint, weak
आलोक m. light
झिलमिलाना vi. to shimmer
डूबना vi. to sink
आकाश m. sky
बेतरतीब adj. disorderly, untidy
क्षण m. moment
ढँकना vi. to be covered

धूप चमक रही थी

धूप f. sunlight
चमकना vi. to shine, to sparkle
और = और
लपकना vi. to catch
मन होना vi. the heart to be inclined
बटोरना vt. to gather, to draw in
उछालना vt. to toss up
बढना vi. to go forward or ahead
अंधकार m. darkness
समेटना vt. to gather up

हल्की-हल्की ला लिमा

लालिमा f. red glow: blush
आकाश m. sky
फेन m. foam
बादल m. cloud
अस्त होना vi. to set (as the sun), to sink
बहना vi. to flow, to float
संग adv. together (with के)
गूँज f. echo, resonance
पुकार f. call, shout

आकाश और आकाश के बीच

आकाश m. space, sky
विभाजन m. division, partition
रेख f. line
पार m. far bank or side
नियति f. fate; obligation
महत्व m. significance
रोशनी f. light, brightness
अँधकार m. darkness
निश्चिति f. settlement; certainty

अंधेरे-सी छा गयी हूं

आकाश m. sky
बरसना vi. to rain
परत f./m. fold
जमना vi. to be collected
बादल m. cloud

पृथ्वी को पैरों तले रौंदता

पृथ्वी f. earth
तले adv. under
रौंदना vt. to trample on, to crush

किलबिलाना vi. to wriggle
टुकड़ा m. piece
फिसलाना vi. to slip, to slide

बच्चे की बाँहों-सा-मचला

बाँह f. the upper arm
मचला adj. stubborn, unruly
मन m. mind, heart, soul
सहमना vi. to be struck with terror
बरौनी f. eyelash
अटकना vi. to linger
तरल adj. tremulous; unsteady
सर्द adj. cold; indifferent; joyless

गो यह सच

गो conj. although
मुट्ठी f. fist, clutch
कसना vt. to draw tight
हथेली f. palm (of the hand)
फैलाना vt. to spread, to expand
बाँधना vt. to tie, to bind
सपना m. dream
समेटना vt. to gather up
पीड़ा f. pain, suffering; sorrow
लुटाना vt. to bring down, to lower
मन m. mind, heart, soul
एकांत m. solitude
गायन m. singing

. . . दुख तो एक गंध

गंध f. smell
फैलना vi. to spread
गंधहीनता f. smell-lessness
निःशंक adj. fearless
उजागर adj. bright, radiant
ढाँकना vt. to conceal, to cover
आकाश m. sky, air
भीड़ f. crowd
क्षण m. moment
सिमटना vi. to be gathered
छितरना vi. to be diffused
निर्बंध adj. free, unbound
सहज adj. natural; unforced
जागना vi. to wake up

पहाड़ कर लेना है पार

पार करना to cross
कुहरा m. mist, fog
छाया f. shadow
गढ़ना vt. to cast, to mould
बढ़ना vi. to advance, to go forward

AMRITA BHARATI

एक चल रही भूमिका

भूमिका f. role
नाटक m. drama, play
यातना f. torment, agony
मंच m. stage
टुकड़ा m. piece, part
प्रवेश करना vt. to enter
खेलना vt. to act (a part), to perform
बारी f. turn, time
दर्शक m. member of audience
पार करना vt. to get across, to pass
प्रेक्षागृह m. theatre
कोढ़ी m. leper
सूत्रधार m. stage manager
चिन्तित adj. worried
पात्र m. character
उतरना vi. to turn out to be: to turn into,
    to become
रंग m. stage
सज्जा f. decoration
मसलन adv. like, for example
मुकुट m. crown
क्रुस m. cross
कील m. nail
जहर m. poison
छिड़कना vi. to sprinkle, to spray
अदालत m. court of law
नगरजन m. townsfolk (नगर town +
    जन people, folk)
मुखबिर m. informer, spy
नेपथ्य m. backstage; the wings
कानून m. law
हवाले करना vt. to entrust
बीचो बीच adv. in the very middle
बेहोश adj. unconscious
पाप m. sin, wickedness

बोझ m. load, burden
झुकना vi. to be bent down
वचनमुक्त adj. speechless (वचन speech + मुक्त free)
नवशा m. map
गोल adj. round, spherical
सरकना vi. to be moved, displaced, to slip
हाथ आना vi. to come to hand
चारों तरफ adv. all around

दूसरा सवाल

झरना vi. to be shed
गलना vi. to waste; to become emaciated
ग्लानि f. aversion, hate
यन्त्रणा f. torment, suffering
इतिहास m. history; account
झाँकना vt. to peep, to peer
प्रकाशित adj. illuminated, lit
कोना m. corner
रोकना vt. to restrain, to suppress
स्वीकार करना vt. to accept
बचना vi. to escape (from से)
आड़ा adj. causing obstruction
खूँटी f. peg
मानो conj. as if
हटना vi. to move away, or aside, to withdraw
असमर्थता f. helplessness
जाहिर करना vt. to reveal
चीखना vi. to scream, to shriek
बटोरना vt. to gather
टुकड़ा m. piece
नियत adj. fixed
अवधि f. set time, period
जुड़ना vi. to be bound
असंख्यता f. countlessness
निरवधि f. limitless: eternal
समष्टिगत adj. collective
धरती f. earth
निश्चल adj. motionless
हथेली f. palm (of the hand)
चढ़ना vt. to climb

वही एका घटना

युग m. age
सदी f. century

चूहा m. rat, mouse
कुतरना vt. to gnaw, to nibble
चीत्कार m. shriek, scream
सुन्न adj. still; silent, speechless

सन्नाटे में दूर तक

सन्नाटा m. stillness
ढेला m. lump, clod (of earth)
आत्मवस्तु f. something which has soul (आत्म- soul + वस्तु thing)
जीवित adj. living, alive
परित्यक्त adj. deserted
पथ m. path, way
संयोग m. coincidence, chance
तय करना vt. to complete (a journey)
झरना to fall, to be shed: to break off
कण m. particle
आसक्ति f. attraction
भाव m. emotion, feeling
संलग्नता f. attachment
जुड़ना vi. to be joined, attached
स्वप्न m. dream
अस्तित्व m. existence
बारी f. turn
छूटना vi. to be left behind, to fall behind
विश्व m. world, universe
रेतीला adj. sandy, gravelly
अन्धड़ m. violent dust storm
मरुस्थल m. desert
तूफानी adj. stormy, turbulent
महासमुद्र m. great ocean
सूना adj. desolate, empty
पग m. step
पूर्ण m. & adj. (a) whole
समेटना vt. to gather up
प्रक्षेपित करना vt. to throw, to hurl
नीरवता f. silence, stillness
व्याप्त adj. pervaded, spread
विस्तृत adj. expanded; extensive
प्रतिभासित adj. illusive
जल-पुष्प m. flower which grows in water (lotus etc.)
पारावार m. ocean, sea
आहट f. the sound of footsteps

मन रुक गया वहाँ

मन m. mind, heart, soul

नित्य adj. eternal, constant
निरन्तर adj. constant
गतिशील adj. moving, dynamic
लय f. rhythm
अनन्तता f. endlessness, boundlessness,
    infinitude

लेकिन

नियत adj. prescribed: ordained
शेष adj. remaining, left over
विनम्र adj. humble, gentle

शब्द की शान्ति में

धरती f. earth
अनुसरण m. following
पथ m. path
रेखा f. line
एक adj. united, undivided
आत्मा f. soul, spirit, self
शिखर m. peak, summit
खाई f. ditch, chasm
मुड़ना vi. to turn
कविता f. poetry
साथ-साथ adv. together

JYOTSNA MILAN

इस तरह होने के बारे में

भूमिका f. role, part
यों adv. in this way
शर्त f. condition

आस्मान

आसमान m. sky, heavens
साल-दर-साल year after year
के पार ppn. through
घुसना vi. to enter
घूमना vi. to turn round

लगातार

दहशत f. fear, terror, dread
गाड़ना vt. to plant
टाँगना vt. to hang
थैला m. large bag, sack

टोपी f. hat
अँगोछा m. towel
थकान f. tiredness; exhaustion

पैर

असमंजस m. hesitation
सोच f. brooding, thinking
चट = चट से adv. instantly
वजह f. cause, reason
कल्पना f. imagination

पीछे

पलटना vi. to turn
पोंछना vt. to wipe (out), to erase
हाथ लगना the hand(s) to be applied to
    task: carefully

तलाश

तलाश f. search
बदरंग adj. dull, faded
चकित adi. astonished
घूमना vi. to wander
सोफा-तख़त m. sofa bed
चटाई f. mat of interwoven leaves or
    bamboo
घेरना vt. to enclose
तमाम adj. entire
आवारा adj. astray
भटकना vi. to roam about

औरत

क्षण m. moment
ईश्वर m. God; lord, master
मर्द m. man; husband
पुकार f. call
दहकना vi. to blaze, to be set aflame
समूचा adj. entire
वजूद m. existence, body, being
पीड़ा f. pain; affliction
बिलबिलाना vi. to feel pain
फेरना vt. to turn away

शब्द

मूँदना vt. to close

घुमाना vt. to cause to revolve
लकीर f. line
घिरना vi. to be enclosed, encircled
शून्य in. void, nothingness
समूचा adj. entire
के खिलाफ़ ppn. against

अर्थ

अर्थ m. purpose, meaning
साबका m. long acquaintance ~ पडना to
    become well acquainted (with, से)
बचना vi. to be left
शरीर m. body
पगना vi. to be soaked, steeped
उधड़ना vi. to become unravelled,
    undone
जूझना vi. to struggle

रात

मुँह अंधेरे adv. before daybreak
नियम m. normal practice
धँसना vi. to penetrate into: to steal into
घुसपैठ f. intrusion: trespassing

मानना vt. to consider
सिकोडना vt. to draw together
गुडा-मुडा adj. crumpled
बचा-ख़चा adj. left over
फैलाना vt. to stretch out

साथ-साथ आइने में

आइना = आईना m. mirror
झाँकना vt. to peep, to spy
आस्मान m. sky
अँतहीन adj. boundless, endless
उजला adj. bright, radiant
धमकी f. threat
इकलौता adj. only, sole, single

वह

केश m. hair: tresses
वस्त्र m. clothes; garment
घुटना m. knee
बांधना vt. to bind, to wrap
बाँह f. arm, upper arm
घिरना vi. to be surrounded, or
    enclosed (by, से): to be embraced

Bibliography

ABRAMS, M. H., 1988 (5th edn): *A glossary of literary terms* (Fort Worth, Chicago etc: Holt, Rinehart and Winston, Inc).

AGRAWAL, KEDARNATH, 1978: *Gulmehandī: Kedārnāth Agravāl kī kavitāē* (Allahabad: Parimal Prakashan).

AGRAWAL, MAHAVIR, (ed.) 1994: *Shamsher: kavi se bare ādmī* (Durga: Shri Prakashan).

AGYEYA (SACHCHIDANANDA VATSYAYAN), 1955: 'Paricay: Sarveśvar Dayāl Saksenā, *Nayī Kavitā 2*, pp. 33–47.

- 1959: 'Hindi literature' in *Contemporary Indian literature: a symposium*, 2nd edn (New Delhi: Sahitya Academy), pp. 78–99.

- 1976: *Signs and silence: selections from the poetry of 'Agyeya'* (Delhi: Simant Publications).

- 1981: *Nīlāmbarī: poems* (Delhi: Clarion Books).

- 1986: *Sadānīrā: sampūrna kavitāē*, 2 vols (Delhi: National Publishing House).

- 1987: *Cunī huī kavitāē* (Delhi: Rajpal and Sons).

- 1996a (ed.): *Tār saptak*, 6th edn (Delhi: Bharatiya Gyanpith).

- 1996b (ed.): *Dūsrā saptak*, 6th edn (Delhi: Bharatiya Gyanpith).

- 1996c (ed.): *Tīsrā saptak*, 6th edn (Delhi: Bharatiya Gyanpith).

BANDOPADHYAYA, MANOHAR. 1994: *Lives and works of great Hindi poets* (Delhi: B.R. Publishing Corporation).

BERMAN, MARSHALL, 1993: *All that is solid melts into air: the experience of modernity* (London & New York: Verso).

BHARATI, AMRITA, 1978: *Maīne nahī likhī kavitā* (Delhi: Pashyanti).

- 1992: *Sannāte mē dūr tak* (Delhi: Bharatiya Gyanpith).

- 2000: *Man ruk gayā vahā* (Pondicherry: Shatabdi Prakashan).

BHARDWAJ, VINOD (ed.), 1998: 'Ek bare lekhak kī prabuddha pahcān', *Jansattā ravivārī*, (6th September issue).

- 1999: *Mere sāksātkār: Kūvar Nārāyan* (Delhi: Kitabghar).

BHATNAGAR, MAHESH, 1976: *Gajānan Mādhav Muktibodh: jīvan aur kāvya* (Delhi: Rajesh Prakashan).

CALINESCU, MATEI 1987: *Five faces of modernity: Modernism, Avant-garde, Decadence, Kitsch, Postmodernism* (Durham: Duke University Press).

CHATURVEDI, RAMSVARUP, 1990: *Nayī kavitāe: ek sāksya* (Allahabad: Lokbharati Prakashan).

– 1998: *Ādhunik kavitā-yātrā* (Allahabad: Lokbharati).

CZEKALSKA, RENATA, 1999: 'The idea and function of free verse in avantgarde Hindi poetry', a paper presented at the Sixth Vishva Hindi Sammelan, 14–18 September, London.

DAS, MUKUL, 1990: 'Ajneya: the poet who makes himself', *New Quest* 81, pp. 143--149.

DHARWADKER, V. & A.K. RAMANUJAN, (eds) 1996: *The Oxford anthology of modern Indian poetry* (Delhi: Oxford University Press).

GAEFFKE, PETER. 1978: *Hindi literature in the twentieth century* (Wiesbaden: Harrassowitz).

GUPTA, JAGDISH, (ed.) 1956: 'Artha kī lay', *Nayī Kavitā*, vol. 3 (Allahabad: Kavita Prakashan), pp. 1–8 and 103–8.

GUPTA, MAITHILISHARAN, 1920: *Bhārat-Bhāratī* (Chirganv: Sahitya Press).

GUPTA, R., et al., 1994: *Nayā saptak* (Allahabad: Lokbharati Prakashan).

JAIN, LAKSHMICHANDRA (ed.), 1965 (2nd edn): *Cād kā mũh terhā hai* (Delhi: Bharatiya Gyanpith).

JAIN, NEMICHANDRA, (ed.) 1980: *Muktibodh racnāvalī*, six vols (Delhi: Rajkamal Prakashan).

KANTA, 1960: *Jo kuch bhī dekhtī hũ* (Hyderabad: Navhind Prakashan).

– 1964: *Samayātī* (Hyderabad: Navhind Prakashan).

– May 1964: 'Bacce kī bā̃hõ sā' *Kalpanā*, p. 61.

KANTA, see PRABHA (ed.) 1995 and 1996a & b.

KHARE, GANESH, 1993: *Muktibodh: vyakti aur pātra* (Allahabad: Shanti Prakashan).

KUMAR, ANJANI, 1988: *Nayī Kavitā kī bhūmikā* (New Delhi: Sharda Prakashan).

LANGE, VICTOR, 1964, 'Introduction' in G. C. Schwebell (ed.), *Contemporary German Poetry* (New York).

LELE, MADHUKAR et al. (eds), undated: *Agyeya apne bāre mẽ: ek sāksātkār* (Delhi: Akashvani Prakashan).

LOTZ, BARBARA, 2001: 'Long poem or unending poem? On the emergence of Muktibodh's 'Andhere mein', *Hindi: Language, discourse, writing*, vol. 2 (1), pp. 91–108.

LUTZE, LOTHAR, (ed. & tr.) 1968: *Hindilyrik der Gegenwart* (Tuebingen: Horst Erdmann Verlag).

– 1985: *Hindi writing in post-colonial India: a study in the aesthetics of literary production* (Delhi: Manohar Publications).

MACHWE, PRABHAKAR. 1991: *Hindī ke sāhitya-nirmātā: 'Agyeya'* (Delhi: Rajpal and Sons).

MANAS, MUKUL DAS, May–June 1990: 'Ajneya: the poet who makes himself', *New Quest* 81, pp. 142–9.

'MANAV', VISHVAMBHAR, 1978: *Nayī Kavitā: naye kavi* (Allahabad: Lokbharati Prakashan).

MATHUR, SHAKUNT, 1960: *Cãdni cũnar* (Allahabad: Sahirva Bhavan Private Limited).

– 1968: *Abhī aur kuch* (Delhi: Gyanpith Prakashan).

– 1990: *Lahar nahī̃ tūtegī* (New Delhi: National Publishing House).

McGREGOR, R.S., 1974: *Hindi literature of the nineteenth and early twentieth centuries* (Wiesbaden: Harrassowitz).

MEHROTRA, ARVIND (tr.), Fall 1974: 'Gajanan Madhav Muktibodh: three poems', *Journal of South Asian Literature*, vol. X (1), pp. 39–43.

– 1992, (ed.): *The Oxford India anthology of twelve modern Indian poets* (Calcutta etc.: Oxford University Press).

MILAN, JYOTSNA, 1989: *Ghar nahī̃*, Delhi: Gyanbharati.

– September 1995: 'Jyotsnā Milan se Jayśankar kī bātcīt' in *Sāksātkār*, pp. 19–38.

– *Apne āge āge*, unpublished manuscript.

MISHRA, SAVITRI, 1989: *Agytya: Sṛjan aur sandarbha* (Allahabad: Pratigya Prakashan).

MISRA, V., 1967 (2nd printing): *Modern Hindi poetry: an anthology* (Bloomington & London: Indiana University Press).

– 1990: *Āj ke lokpriya Hindi kavi: 'Agyeya'* (Delhi: Rajpal & Sons).

MUKTIBODH, see Ashok Vajpeyi (ed.)

MUKTIBODH, see Lakshmichandra Jain (ed.)

MUKTIBODH, see Trilochan Shastri (ed.)

MUNSHI, VIJAY (tr.), 1989: *Poems: Sarveshwar Dayal Saxena* (Calcutta: Writers Workshop).

- (tr.) 1996: *Cranes in the drought* (Delhi: Sahitya Academy).

NARAIN, KUNWAR, 1989a (4th edn): *Parives̱: ham tum* (Delhi: Vani Prakashan).

- 1989b (4th edn): *Apne sāmne* (Delhi: Rajkamal Prakashan).

- 1996 (2nd print): *Koī dūsrā nahī̃* (Delhi: Rajkamal Prakashan).

- 1998: *Āj aur āj se pahle* (Delhi: Rajkamal Prakashan).

NARAIN, KUNWAR, see Vinod Bhardwaj 1999.

OFFREDI, M., 2001: 'A note on modern Hindi poetry', paper presented at the 2nd International Conference on Indian Studies, Cracow, 19–23 September.

PANDEY, INDU PRAKASH, 1975: *Hindi literature: trends and traits* (Calcutta: Firma K.L. Mukhopadhyay).

PANT, SUMITRANANDAN, 1966 (9td edn): *Rasmibandha* (Delhi: Rajkamal Prakashan).

PATHAK, SHRIDAR, 1918: *Bhārat-gī* (Allahabad: Hindi Sahitya Sammelan).

PRABHA (ed.), 1995: *Kāntā-gītsmṛti* (Bombay: Am Prakashan).

- 1996a: *Kāntā-smṛti: kāvyākār: ek* (Bombay: Am Prakashan).

- 1996b: *Kāntā-smṛti: kāvyākār: do* (Bombay: Am Prakashan).

RAGHUVAMSHA October 1963: 'Śamśer–aindrajālik kavi', *Kalpanā*, pp. 56–70.

RAMAKRISHNAN, E.V., (ed.) 1999: *The tree of tongues: an anthology of modern Indian poetry* (Shimla: Indian Institute of Advanced Studies).

RAV, BALKRISHNA, 1965: 'Kũvar Nārāyan: paricay', *Nayī Kavitā 3*, pp. 26–47.

RAY, RAJKAMAL, 1986: *Śikhar se sāgar tak: Agyeya kī jīvan yātrā* (Delhi: National Publishing House).

RAY, RAMKAMAL, 1997: *Nayī Kavitā: nayī dṛsti* (Allahabad: Hindustani Academy).

RICHARDS, I.A., 1991 (first published 1929): *Practical criticism* (London: Routledge).

ROSENSTEIN, 1993: 'Sacetan Kahānī and Samāntar Kahānī–Principal movements in the Hindi short story of the 1960s and 1970s', *South Asia Research*, vol. 13 (2), pp. 117–31.

- 2000: '"New poetry" in Hindi: A quest for modernity', *South Asia Research*, vol. 20 (1), pp. 47–62.

- 2001: 'Shakespeare's sister in India: In search of Hindi women poets' *Hindi: Language, Discourse, Writing*, vol. 1 (3–4), pp. 47–87.

RUBIN, DAVID, 1993: *The Return of Sarasvati: Translations of the poetry of Prasad, Nirala, Pant and Mahadevi* (Philadelphia: University of Pennsylvania).

SAHAY, RAGHUVIR. 1959: 'Savyākhyā–Raghuvīr Sahāy, *Nayī Kavitā 4*,   pp. 32–41.

– 1985 (3rd edn): *Ātmahātyā ke viruddha* (Delhi: Rajkamal Prakashan).

– 1989a (3rd edn): *Log bhūl gaye hai* (Delhi: Rajkamal Prakashan).

– 1989b: *Kuch pate kuch citthiyā̃* (Delhi: Rajkamal Prakashan).

– 1997 (2nd edn): *Sīṛhiyõ par dhūp mẽ* (Delhi: Vani Prakashan).

SAHAY, see Senkevich (tr.)

SAHAY, see Suresh Sharma (ed.)

SATCHIDANANDAN, K., (ed.) 2000: *Signatures: one hundred Indian poets* (Delhi: National Book Trust).

SAXENA, SARVESHWAR DAYAL, 1966: *Ek sūnī nāv* (Delhi: Akshar Prakashan Ltd.).

– 1994 (2nd edn): *Jangal kā dard* (Delhi: Rajkamal Prakashan).

SAXENA, see Prayag Shukla (ed.)

SCHOMER, K., 1983: *Mahadevi Varma and the Chhayavad age of modern Hindi poetry* (Berkeley etc.: University of California Press).

SENKEVICH, ALEKSANDR (TR.), 1983: *Raghuvir Sahai: Izbrannoe* (Moscow: Molodaya Gvardiya).

SHAH RAMESHCHANDRA, 1990: *Bhārtīya sāhitya ke nirmātā: Agyeya* (Delhi: Sahitya Academy),

– 1994: 'Poised vulnerability: *Koi doosra nahin* by Kunvwar Narayan', *The Book Review*, vol. XVIII, No 5, pp. 7–8.

SHARATKUMAR, et al. (interviewers), 1988: *Racnā: kyõ aur kin ke bic [Agyga se kuch samvād]* (Merath: Bharatiya Sahitya Prakashan).

SHARMA, SURESH, (ed.) 1994: *Raghuvīr Sahāy: Pratinidhi kavitāẽ* (Delhi: Rajkamal Paperbacks).

SHASTRI, TRILOCHAN, (ed.) 1991: *Muktibodh kī kavitāẽ* (Delhi: Sahitya Academy).

SHRIVASTAV, P., (ed.) 1993 (3rd edn): *Kedārnāth Singh: Pratinidhi kavitaẽ* (Delhi: Raikamal Paperbacks).

SHUKLA, PRAYAG, (ed.) 1996 (4th edn): *Sarveśvardayāl Saksenā: Pratinidhi kavitaẽ* (Delhi: Rajkamal Paperbacks).

SINGH, GITA, 2000: 'Kavayitrī Kāntā: Śabdakarma', MPhil dissertation, Hyderabad University.

SINGH, KEDARNATH, 1990 (2nd edn): *Akāl mẽ sāras* (Delhi: Rajkamal Prakashan).

- 1995a (3rd edn): *Yahā̃ se dekho* (Delhi: Radhakrishna).

- 1995b: *Uttar Kabīr aur anya kavitāẽ* (Delhi: Rajkamal Prakashan).

- 1996: *Bāgh* (Delhi: Bharatiya Gyanpith).

KEDARNATH SINGH, see P. Shrivastav (ed.)

KEDARNATH SINGH, see V. Munshi. 1996

SINGH, NAMWAR (ed.), 1994 (2nd edn): *Shamsher Bahadur Singh: Pratinidhi Kavitāẽ* (Delhi: Rajkamal Paperbacks).

- 1997 (4th edn): *kavitā ke naye pratimān* (Delhi: Rajkamal Prakashan).

- 2001: 'Andhere Mein': Searching for the ultimate expression', *Hindi: Language, discourse, writing*, vol. 2 (1), pp. 109–118.

SINGH, SHAMSHER BAHADUR, January 1958: Lekhak kī notbuk se: 1952–1955 se cune hue vividh amś, *Kalpanā*, p. 52.

- December 1964: 'Dāyrī ke panne', *Kalpanā*, p. 63.

- 1988: *Kāl tujhse hor hai merī* (Delhi: Vani Prakashan).

SINGH, SHAMSHER BAHADUR, see Namwar Singh (ed.)

SNELL, RUPERT, 1991: *The Hindi classical tradition: a Braj Bhāṣā reader* (London: SOAS).

- 1993: 'Agyeya translates Agyeya: the Nīlāmbarī poems', *India International Centre Quarterly*, vol. 20 (4), pp. 109–128.

STORR, ANTHONY, 1988: *Solitude: a return to the self* (New York: Ballantine Books).

VAJPEYI, ASHOK, 1994 (4th edn): *Gajanan M. Muktibodh: Pratinidhi kavitāẽ* (Delhi: Rajkamal Paperbacks).

VAJPEYI, KAILASH, (ed.) 1998: *An anthology of modern Hindi poetry* (Delhi: Rupa & Co).

VARMA, URMILA, 1980: *Influence of English Poetry on Modern Hindi Poetry (1900–1940) with special reference to technique, imagery, metre and diction* (Allahobad: Lokbharati Prakashan)

VATSYAYAN, SACHCHIDANDA, see Agyeya.

WEISSBORT, DANIEL & ARVINDA MEHROTRA, (eds), 1993: *Periplus: poetry in translation* (Delhi: Oxford University Press).

WEISSBORT, DANIEL & GIRIDHAR RATHI (eds), 1994: *Survival: an experience and an experiment in translating modern Hindi poetry* (Delhi: Sahitya Academy).

ZIDE, ARLENE, (ed.) 1993: *In their own voice: the Penguin anthology of contemporary Indian women poets* (Penguin Books India).

Journals

All specific references to material published in journals is listed under the author's name in the general bibliography. Only general references to journals are included in this section.

Hindi: Language, discourse, writing, vol. 1 (3–4), October 2000–March 2001. focus on Shamsher Bahadur Singh, Singh, R. (ed.).

Hindi: Language, discourse, writing, vol. 2 (1), April–June 2001, focus on Muktibodh, Singh, R. (ed.).

Indian horizons, vol. 42, *Bees of the invisible: poems from India,* a special issue, 1993,Vajpeyi, A. (ed.).

Indian literature 153, January–February 1993, focus on Hindi poetry, Satchidanandan (ed.).

Indian literature 180, July–August 1997, focus on women's poetry, Satchidanandan (ed.).

Yārā, 1996, a special issue on women's writing, Bhalla, A. (ed.), Gill, G. (guest ed.).

CPSIA information can be obtained at www.ICGtesting.com
Printed in the USA
LVOW070820261212

313226LV00002B/49/P